SICK AND TIRED
OF BEING
SICK AND TIRED

SICK AND TIRED

OF BEING

SICK AND TIRED

Bill Schlondrop

This book was printed in the United States of America.

To order additional copies of this book, contact:
Xlibris Corporation
1-888-7-XLIBRIS
www.Xlibris.com
Orders@Xlibris.com

CONTENTS

BOOK ONE

BOOK TWO

BOOK THREE

TO ALL MY FRIENDS WHO ARE FRIENDS OF BILL W.

INTRODUCTION

This story is not an all-encompassing solution for every aspect of recovery from the Disease of Alcoholism. It is however, my understanding of how my recovery manifested itself from my own unique approach, based upon many years of studying and trying. It is very difficult to recover from any addiction. But with help, people can and do recover. It took me nine years before I wrote this book. Part of the reason was simply that I didn't want to offend anybody, and partly because I had to convince myself that I could maintain a reasonable period of positive recovery prior to writing it. Notice that I said *recovery*, instead of *sobriety*. There is a significant difference between the two words.

During three attempts at recovery, I've interviewed hundreds of patients, and many counselors in several hospitals and recovery centers. I have had considerable time to do research, and if there is such an award, believe that I qualify for a Ph.D. in Alcohol Recovery. A key element to recovery is that the person must **want** it. There can be no successful recovery without this desire. Yet, to my knowledge, there aren't many rehabilitation centers out there that use this approach.

In the real world, the one we live in today, the term, drugs, carries with it a respectable negativity. To free us from some type of pain, be it real or imagined, some people rely on the use of drugs as a coping mechanism. This pain includes fear of the unknown. For addicts, this is the fear of change. Under the cloud of the all-protective cover of alcohol, a pseudo-reality exists within a small portion of the mind that causes a distrust of everyone, except us, and those like us. We are faced with a paradox. Our enemy is not the substance, but it has become the syndrome whereby our addiction is created. Media addiction is one of the best examples. Watching television makes life bearable for most people who spend hours in front of the tube. This problem can be solved simply be turning off a switch. But where is the switch that shuts off the casual circumstances of drinking that leads to alcohol addiction?

Most patients, because of their addiction, have been loners, spending most or all of their time under the influence of their drug of choice, and running away from other people. This usually begins with running from, or avoiding people in authority, but as the effects of the drugs progress, involves all persons, including loved ones. In the three recovery centers that I attended, the one glaring omission most patients all agreed on was the lack of any supporting family atmosphere to help overcome their fear. The paradox with alcoholism is that the disease keeps telling us it isn't a disease. It tells us it simply is a source of relief. And herein lies the problem.

To live in a new, sober world, we need to know it. During early recovery, we are subjected to biological, or phantom functions called emotions. These emotions control our mental state, and any dangers here can result in the fundamental mechanism called fear. Fear is a powerful motivator for our future behaviors, especially where a long-term achievement such as a recovery program is concerned.

An alcoholic probably has spent years avoiding everyone, while going to great lengths to cover up the very act of his or her drinking: Drinking before going to parties so as to keep the intake in front of witnesses low. Then leaving early, to be able to drink heavily without anyone watching, hence the term, "a closet drinker". Drinking prior to scheduled meetings, particularly when active participation is involved. Drinking to go to sleep. You get the idea. Suddenly, in a treatment center, all these secrets will be revealed. On top of this, withdrawal sets in, and the mind and body scream for relief, . . . in the form of a much needed drink. We have grown accustomed to the relief and protection from alcohol, and fear any change. In no place is this misunderstood fear felt at a greater level than in the newly recovering alcoholic.

And it knows no boundaries. The patient, new to treatment, dreams up a wide scope of fearful fantasies concerning his or her condition and outlook. In fact, the fear for some of the patients I spoke with was so great, that it prompted me to write a story about the supposed maltreatment, *totally untrue*, of the unsavory atmosphere these patients actually believed existed in one recovery center. I've included the story here to illustrate how great the level of fear can be in some patients' minds, and to give an idea of the monumental problems faced by patients early in their recovery program.

I wrote the story while a patient in a recovery center. It was published in *The Story Shop VI, Rio Grande Press,* in 1998, where it won the Editor's Choice Award.

NOT A TRUE STORY

Guinea Pig

SIM 4863 lay motionless under stiff white sheets on an iron bed with locked wheels. Beneath his paper thin skin, blue veins showed watery blood barely pulsing from a heart driven by a pacemaker. A strong healthy body fifteen days ago, now reduced to a pile of waxy skin and bones.

A faint reddish glow permeated each silent room. The only movement, the monitor traces sweeping across displays, or the slowly dripping IV feeders.

In the hallway, the steady, but hushed squeak of Nurse Mates broke the silence. Strong-muscled legs moved the shoes at a determined pace as they had done often in the past whenever nurse Audrey Meghan made rounds. Youthful-looking, with fair skin and silver-gray hair trimmed short but full, her soft green eyes allowed her face to resemble that of a child.

As misuse of drugs and alcohol continued to rise, Residential Substance Abuse Recovery Centers became increasingly popular. More and more people entered treatment for one reason or another: court ordered, family pressured, or by career ultimatums. Audrey had been working at this center as Head Nurse and counselor for six years. She entered the room, stopped by the foot of the bed, and gazed at the clipboard hanging over the end.

Anonymity is a valued tenet among recovering alcoholics. All patients had their identity indicated by the first three letters in their last name, and the last four numbers of their social security identification. She knew SIM 4863 personally.

Two years ago, SIM 4863 had entered the protected confines of the Residential Recovery Center. A tall, thick man, beer-bellied and rheumy-eyed, his brusk and demanding manner remained the only remnants of his military career. After 45 years of hard drinking and substance abuse, he had entered this treatment center much the same as everyone else. Full of denial, angry, and depressed, he knew his problem, and exactly how his treatment should be administered.

Not until he had been enrolled in the program five weeks did he begin accepting his dilemma. As happened with most patients, he started responding to treatment after detoxification and the loss of some of the poisons in him. Once acceptance became a familiar feeling to him, his recovery progress soared. He became more humble, sought help with all the things he didn't understand, and eagerly pursued his rehabilitation program.

Sometimes it's best to release yourself from attachments you've had for a long time, and begin a fresh start, his counselor advised. This presented his first significant hurdle, divorce as he interpreted it. After 33 years of marriage, he took the big step. He hadn't been sure it was the right thing to do, but his counselor assured him that his recovery came first. How many times had he heard that phrase?

His next two hurdles came together: *Never have a relationship with someone of the opposite sex until you have been clean for at least two years,* and *Never, never have a relationship, no matter how small, with any of your therapists or counselors.* These he disregarded.

"I never thought this would happen to me," he said one night. "I tried to condition myself that feelings for another would be beyond me as long as I maintained my steadfast approach to keeping clean."

"When you have so much love and tenderness inside," his partner responded, "it's only normal for you to want to be able to share it with someone."

He gave in and quickly became deeply involved with another

person. He lived for her, and lived his program for her. He forgot one other main factor. They had told him over and over again, *You can't get sober, you can't stay clean, for anyone or anything other than yourself.*

He didn't care.

Then impotence reared its ugly head.

"You had so many poisons inside you," his partner consoled, "you can't expect to have everything readjust to normal in an instant. Give it time."

He gave it time. He gave it more than time. He tried to hasten things by artificially inducing the urge and the results. He spent thousands of dollars on pills, mechanical devices, books, and cures. Against his doctor's advice, he took the mail-order medication knowing significant damage might result to his already diseased liver. He stopped visiting his family and seeing his friends, who by now, noticing his recovery improvement, offered considerable support to his progress. He no longer went to AA meetings.

"It's going to be all right," his partner kept telling him. "Sex isn't always the most important thing within a relationship. You'll come back around to being normal soon enough."

After a while, he did notice a slight change in his ability. He couldn't be certain whether it came from the exercise, the pills, the mechanical devices, his determination, a combination of them all, or just the fact that by now his body had finally rid itself of most of the poisons.

"See, I told you things would start getting better," his partner said one day. "You'll be normal before you know it."

Being normal. What was normal? He thought about this constantly. Had his life been normal before when he continuously used and drank all the time? He had done some significant things; raised a family of four, made a reasonable salary, and even attained his retirement dream, property with a river view.

To be normal, did it mean failing, then admitting and accepting, and finally turning oneself around, and trying to fix things? If that was the case, he qualified as being more normal now, as an admitted addict and free from drugs, than he had ever been previously. These things had never been properly explained to him. Perhaps they couldn't be explained.

While working his program, his nervous system had worn thinner than he ever remembered. Even when completely under the influence of his drug of choice he had managed to feel better than he sometimes felt in the early days of his recovery. How many times in the past had he been tempted to chuck the whole recovery program, to just return to the wonderful arena where a quick drink or snort would solve all his troubles?

But he stayed in there, and things would be all right he said over and over. He started going to meetings again. But some things he still didn't understand.

For example, he didn't realize that during treatment, a person takes only a few days to get sober, but residual poison levels remain for years. During this time, the same person, if lucky, will discover the approach needed to rebuild a new self. It is a renascence, a new birth. Since he had broken the rules, however, he never developed a solid and practical approach to his recovery program. He felt, but didn't accept, that it takes the rest of a person's life to recover; to learn to accept life on life's terms, to live life on a daily basis. Indeed, live moment-by-moment, even breath-by-breath if necessary, in order to prevent a relapse. Once willingness, open-mindedness, and honesty take hold, recovery becomes easier. There is light at the tunnel's end, and rewards as well, but a person must want to recover above all else.

There is a caveat–something else he didn't know–which to him would be the worst mistake he would ever make. His final, and deadliest hurdle came one night after he returned from a meeting and went to kiss his partner.

"What's that on your lip?" she asked. "Right by the side of your mouth. What is it?"

"It's an old wart I've had for years," he answered. "You must have noticed it before."

"Well," she yelled, "until you get rid of that thing, you're not going to kiss me. I think it's a condyloma, and that's a sexually transmitted disease."

He extended his arms, palms up.

"But, I've had it for years."

"No matter," she said, her raised voice clipping the words. "You're not going to touch me again until you get that thing taken care of."

He remained motionless as she stormed out of the room.

Sure enough, his doctor confirmed the lesion as being a condyloma, but not necessarily a sexually transmitted disease.

He tried to explain, but she remained adamant and unrelenting, he could no longer touch her. He could no longer kiss the woman he loved.

In the Marines he had a saying: *If you pull a Guinea Pig's tail hard enough, its eyes will fall out.* The answer to the riddle is that these little animals have no tails. However, the words, Guinea Pig, are also associated with anything used for experimenting. He never realized then that the saying would come back and kill him.

Nurse Meghan weighed his predicament over in her mind as she stood gazing at the lifeless form on the bed. She knew that alcohol and cocaine addiction are progressive diseases that continue to build a craving within the body after the addicted person stops the intake.

If a person has had a long history of addiction, then stops for several years, and begins using or drinking again, a peculiar thing happens. The new intake does not revert to the small doses initially sufficient to cause the feelings of euphoria and well-being. The quantity now needed to provide the necessary stimulus is not even what it had been when the user stopped. Instead, it is an additional amount, an amount that would have been reached if the person had not stopped at all! The partly rehabilitated body cannot stand the terrible onslaught of invading drugs. Metabolism is insufficient, and the organs of the body quickly deteriorate. The result is a very rapid decline of all internal life support mechanisms. It happens in a period of several weeks. It is merciless, agonizingly quick, very painful, and deadly.

Her gaze moved to the foot of the bed, and to the chart on the clipboard–the DNR box had been checked–do not resuscitate! Yes, she knew this patient well. She had been aware of the risk taken when he disregarded the advice not to become involved before the two-year period. She also knew the risk taken when he said he planned to go back out, that he could handle it now. Besides, he had said it remained the only thing left for him.

But what about therapists and counselors? Aren't they allowed to lead normal lives within which relationships occur and perhaps continue? What about those friendships that could lead to commitments? She quickly broke that train of thought.

She knew that SIM 4863's present condition did not result from the terrible aftermath of an unwanted relapse. She knew he had planned this suicide.

Nurse Meghan walked back to her office, and slumped heavily into her chair. Each long day took its toll. Most of her colleagues said their daily routines could be simply sloughed off at the close of work, and that they returned home and went about their own lives in a normal manner. She suspected otherwise.

Dr. Andsaca, the resident psychologist, and Chief of the center entered with a stack of new records.

He walked up behind her, bent over, and kissed her neck. She shivered at his touch, her hands gripping the keyboard tray.

"You're looking a little tired, sweetheart," he said. "Is everything all right?"

"Yes," she said. She did not turn to look at him.

"Well," he said, putting the records on her desk, "you certainly did a marvelous job with this last patient, I want you to know that. Here are some files of new patients I think may prove promising. Three more, and we'll be ready to publish."

As he left the room, he said over his shoulder, "Take off early tonight, if you think you need it."

"Thank you," she said, never taking her eyes from the blank monitor screen.

She powered up her computer. While it booted up, that is,

loaded the automatically executed programs, she glanced at the stack of new patient folders.

Guinea Pigs.

The automatic boot up finished, and the screen presented a file. She began the closeout on SIM 4863.

AGAIN, THIS WAS NOT A TRUE STORY

I believe that the greatest fear does not come at the beginning of treatment, when only a small number of people will know of the alcoholic's situation. Instead, I feel that it comes at the time of release from treatment. The patient, now clean and sober, but still suffering from the disease of alcoholism, is turned loose to face society alone. The black cloud, the stigma of having been in treatment, and having been labeled an alcoholic, is the ultimate fear.

There is an enormous misunderstanding about the disease of alcoholism and its recovery programs. It exists on the side of the patients, as well as on the side of the professional personnel involved in recovery therapy. This begs the question, Does the system actually give the patient the tools to follow a successful recovery program?

My story, *Sick and Tired of Being Sick and Tired*, is autobiographical. It discusses some of the areas I felt to be causal in most of the misunderstandings that I discovered. The plot shows how a person can grow from hostility to charitableness, from pretentiousness to humility, and finally, and most important for recovering people, from denial to acceptance. Remember that I said a key word in anyone's recovery is *want*.

I hope you enjoy and learn something from the story.

BOOK ONE

Sick and Tired
of Being
Sick and Tired

1

The Fledgling

"Yes sir, Gunner," the corporal said again. "The Adjutant said very specifically that you had been scheduled to run the Physical Readiness Test at oh-six hundred hours Monday morning." He saluted, executed an about face smartly, and continued about his other business.

Reality had finally caught up with Chief Warrant Officer Bill S. He shut the door to his quarters, sat, sipped his martini, and thought about what the conveyed information meant. Several things became clear at once: Monday would be here in two more days, and in no way would he be in shape to run the PRT. At forty-three, after almost twenty-four years in the Marines, he had become his own victim of too much vacillation, too much dodging of the important military stuff, and too much booze. This type of situation had been occurring more frequently lately. He became frightened.

He rose, strode to the counter, and poured another, larger martini. He would have to think this one out. He did not want to suffer any embarrassment by making a miserable and futile attempt trying to pass the test. Everyone would be there watching, and he didn't want to fall flat on his face, probably literally. He drank and thought and drank some more until Sunday night, finally reaching a decision—he would again, take the easy way out, and buy some time. He made a phone call.

"Colonel, this is Gunner S, I believe I have a candidate for the squadron's drug abuse program."

Oddly enough, the colonel, when he heard, seemed to understand, and invited him to his quarters to talk about it. The colonel said he was surprised when Bill admitted that he was the candidate.

"I never suspected," the colonel said. Was he being polite?

He gave Bill some soft drinks, encouraged him to stick with them for the remainder of the night, and told him to report to the squadron's doctor first thing in the morning.

Early the next morning, Bill received a cursory examination by the doctor, and was told to sit and wait in the hall for transportation to the US Naval Hospital, Camp Kui, Okinawa. He wasn't allowed to first go by his quarters to pick up clothes and shaving gear. The doctor no doubt suspected Bill would also pick up several drinks as well.

The Marine Corps' drug abuse program, new at the time, meant nobody knew much about it. Neither did the US Navy apparently, but somebody had seen the movie, *Lost Weekend*, and foresaw violent scenes of withdrawal and hallucinations coming from one patient, CWO Bill S. Therefore, they put him in the "Psych Ward," which had metal bars around all the doors and windows, and placed him under heavy sedation. It was while he was here, that he became aware of the strange, defamatory stigma, usually associated with mental health patients. He spent five days under sedation of "legal" drugs, not remembering much.

His commanding officer paid one visit, probably as a required courtesy, and the remainder of the time Bill spent alone.

He did remember trying to shave with the razor they issued him at certain times. It had a lock in the handle, to keep from getting to the blade, and a rake-like covering that prevented the blade from being used as a deadly instrument, for wrist slashing, and the like, he supposed. Someone watched him the entire time he had the instrument in his hands. He did remember that the device didn't shave very well.

They allowed him to participate in some creative arts. This meant that he could use crayons to color items he created out of stiff paper.

He made a little toy soldier, colored the uniform bright blue, and with a string, suspended the model from a light chain above his bed. He had a significant amount of difficulty getting a scissors to cut out the shape initially, but managed to convince his monitors that he wouldn't attempt serious or life-threatening action with the instrument. It had been a child's scissors with rounded tips and dull blades.

On the morning of the sixth day, still groggy, although his medication had been stopped, his doctor said, "We have done all we can do for you here, your liver profile values are nearly normal, and you should be getting better. You are to go to building four immediately behind this hospital."

Bill did as directed.

"Why are you coming here?" the fat civilian seated behind the desk asked him.

"I was told to come here, I've been released from the fourth floor," Bill said.

"Why are you here?"

"I told you," Bill said. "I was being treated for alcohol abuse, and have just been released from the fourth floor of the hospital."

"But why are you here?"

This was getting old.

Somewhat irritated, Bill started over again.

"Look, I just told you twice. I was being treated for alcohol abuse and . . ."

The fat civilian rose from his seat, and waddled out from behind his desk.

"You're not answering the question," he yelled disgustedly. "You're supposed to be asking for help."

Bill didn't like civilians too much anyway, let alone fat ones who harassed him, and gave the impression that they didn't like recovering people. He raised his voice to out shout the fat civilian, and again went through the ritual of trying to explain to this person why he had come through the door.

"I did ask for help. I went to my commanding officer six days ago and . . ."

This building functioned as a Halfway House, but Bill S had never heard of one. He would not understand the purpose of Halfway Houses until many years later. So far, he had been subjected to a treatment period called detoxification. This had consisted of prescribed drugs to help him over the transition period, while the poisons from all his drinking left his body.

He had been given two choices from the fat civilian: Stay here for five more months in an ongoing recovery program, or return to his unit, and attend local Alcoholics Anonymous meetings there. Figuring he would be shot if he stayed away five months, CWO Bill S opted for the new world of AA meetings.

Immediately after reporting to his unit, he put in his request to retire. He didn't know it at the time, but this would be his first attempt at recovery by using the popular, but unsuccessful, geographical changes cure. If you can't drive the bus, go to another location.

His commanding officer told him that all the officers had been notified of the reason he had been in the hospital, but not the enlisted men. They had been informed that he had gone for surgery on his legs. A sympathetic cover up that he noted would occur many times in later life. Once his replacement arrived, he acquired the job of SLJO (Shitty Little Jobs Officer) by Bill's own definition.

Throughout history, whenever a Marine unit had an unruly body, or one suspected of an offense that might result in disciplinary action, that person received verbal orders to report to the Chaplain for "rehabilitation". The Chaplain issued dust rags, and had the Marine polish the chapel. The SLJO had an office in a small building behind the Chaplain's office. Now, all the Marines being held in administrative hold for various reasons reported here, to Bill, every day.

These troops could not be permitted to loll around the barracks or the PX, since it would create animosities among the straight Marines. Neither could this unruly bunch be allowed to follow a normal work routine, since they had been labeled dissidents, and their constant bitching would corrupt the pure. It only took twenty of these dissidents, under Bill's supervision, one hour to make the chapel spotless. Then, they retired to the small building behind the chapel, and discussed their situations.

The AA meetings he attended proved to be of no help to Bill's program. Six Marines from the immediate area, all male, attended these meetings, Bill being the only officer. The group had the standard AA text called The Big Book, copies of the Twelve Steps, and several supporting handouts. Meetings consisted of each recovering person sitting around a table, in a room with paper walls over a Japanese tavern, and relating what his past had been like. For four months, each Tuesday and Thursday, at twenty-hundred hours, Bill attended the meetings while the recovering Marines told their stories over and over. He noticed that the stories increased in impact, intensity, and surreptitious content each time they would be related.

Whining and crying seemed to prevail. All present considered themselves victims, blaming anything and everybody, but them-selves for their condition. One blamed his drinking on an over-powering sexual urge, another because he didn't possess enough sexual drive. The rest blamed the Marine Corps. The disease con-cept of alcoholism never came up, and no person attended who had a significant amount of recovery time to impart any wisdom. The blind continued to lead the blind.

There has to be a better way, what am I learning?

The SLJO came under the supervision of the squadron's S-1 officer. The S-1 office provided the administrative functions, and became involved with those Marines implicated in disci-plinary actions. Bill, of course, received the task of investigating all related incidents.

If a Marine had been picked up, and the Military Police found any kind of pill on his person, aspirin or otherwise, that individual immediately would be placed on administrative hold while an in-vestigation followed. The pill, or pills, was sent to Tokyo for analy-sis, and turnaround time could be six months or more. In the process of investigating, Bill found that the young Marines related to him, because he admitted up front to his alcoholism, but they remained suspicious since he represented authority by virtue of his warrant officer rank. They even listened to, and heeded some of what he told them, but this slight change in his acceptance still didn't enter his own mind. This became the first time Bill sensed a fear from men who had been put in a defensive position concerning their drug habits. Many years later, Bill would finally realize that truth in his dealings would provide a tremendous boost to him, and to those people with whom he dealt.

'   CWO Bill S uncovered a Marine Corps Order that addressed substance abuse, and found that money had been allocated for this purpose. He ordered films, movie projectors, books, pamphlets, and handouts covering various aspects of rehabilitative recovery programs. He and his crew began learning about recovery.

From time to time, Marines qualified in the instruction of a new program, called Human Relations, would arrive on the island, and conduct formal training classes. These classes included some training in recognizing problems associated with drug abuses. Discussion and critique sessions followed each class, supervised by the formally trained Marines, usually staff NCOs, but Bill S didn't learn enough. And he didn't take anything with him when his tour ended, either on his person or in his mind. Perhaps he hadn't been ready, and perhaps he hadn't really wanted to.

He didn't realize it at the time, but because he had stopped drinking, the performance level of his daily routines escalated considerably.

"You do such good work," the S-1 officer told him one day, "I wish I had a dozen of you. After you turn in a report, there is nothing left for us to do but simply forward it. Keep up the good work."

This should have been a lesson for Bill, but it never entered his mind that his past performances might have been impaired because of his drinking. Bill's mind had been conditioned by alcohol for so long that whatever he did, always seemed to him anyway, to be the best that he had to offer. Indeed, he felt his performance to be exemplary in most cases. How far could he have gone, and what other great things might he have been able to do, had his mind not been clouded with alcohol? He had received no training in this area of recovery, so he never thought about it.

On the day Bill had been driven to the airport, they stopped by his replacement's quarters.

"There's the bar," CWO Bob said, "help yourself."

"But I really shouldn't," Bill S replied, "I'm doing real well on this attempt at sobriety."

"What the hell do you care now?" Bob said. "You never drank all that much, and these people will never see you again anyway. Once you're a civilian, that easy living will take away all your stress, and you'll have no trouble controlling your drinking."

CWO Bill S, newly converted teetotaler, had three gin and tonics prior to the trip to the airport. On the plane flight home he had more.

It came as a shock when Bill S discovered that the world had not stopped as a result of his brief attempt at sobriety. Halfway Houses are geared to help in making the difficult transition of adopting a sober life easier, but alas, his first introduction to one had failed miserably. Up to this point he hadn't received any counseling at all. The geographical change, and the induction into the chaotic world of misguided civilians, only added to the stress for newly retired, now Captain, Bill S.

Upon retirement, reinstatement of highest rank held had helped, but with twenty-four years of military regimentation ingrained within, the conditions of the outside world still seemed for Bill S to be "too far to the main gate with nobody in charge". None of these conditions contributed to helping Bill S maintain any kind of sobriety.

2

Still Looking

Bill S had been retired from the Marines for eight years when it became necessary for him to seek treatment a second time. Becoming necessary meant being offered a choice by his employer–either participate in the treatment program or be fired.

He had done rather well working for this huge defense contractor since his retirement. To Bill, it had simply meant doing the same type of job he had done in the Marines, only now he could wear civvies. In spite of the alcohol, he had earned a highly respectable level of expertise on the missile system he would be involved with for almost forty-two years.

Some things still remained the same. For instance, he still felt the requirement to drink half a quart of vodka prior to any heavy briefing commitment, usually for high-priced individuals like generals. All practicing alcoholics had undying faith in the false belief that vodka did not leave one's breath subject to detection. Besides, he usually stayed on the stage behind the lectern, and some distance from anyone who might smell the alcohol on his breath. Breath mints, gum, and peanuts served to cover anything detectable in situations that required closer proximity.

Sometimes working in the field for extended periods of time proved to be difficult from the standpoint of having to do without alcohol. He developed a ruse that worked nicely. Instead of taking soft drinks in cans to the field with him, he brought bottles with screw caps. He would drain some of the soda from some of the bottles, refill them with vodka, and mark the tops with a small mark from a ball point pen. That way he could identify the spiked bottles from the clear, and could offer someone else a drink without giving away his secret. He always remembered to keep the trunk of his vehicle locked: It contained textbooks, test equipment, tools, and his cooler.

Long driving distances didn't phase him in the least. He had learned from a colleague that by simply filling the windshield wiper container with vodka, and then disconnecting the hose, and leading it inside to an area near the steering column, this afforded easy access to alcohol whenever in transit, without drawing any undue attention from outside. Besides, in Texas, where he now lived and worked, everyone drank beer while driving, as an unofficial state symbol. Cops didn't seem to mind, and if your pick up bed didn't have smashed, empty beer cans in it, you didn't belong.

It had come as somewhat of a shock to his alcoholic brain when, after two replacements had to be provided in order to finish his latest tasks, the seemingly severe option concerning the recovery program had been issued. He actually thought he had been doing a good job. The way it was put might have had something to do with it.

"We want you to take some time off, and participate in a drug and alcohol abuse recovery program," he had been told. "So far, seven of our senior instructors, and three managers have been sent to this program, and they are all doing fine. We think it's time for you to go." Put to him that way, he couldn't refuse. Besides, he needed the job.

Since his first unsuccessful attempt at recovery, he had harbored a deep resentment as to the acquired effectiveness of any kind of recovery program. He felt that he hadn't learned a thing. But then, that first attempt had only lasted six days. This program would be for twenty-eight days, almost five times as long. He should have a much better chance of learning something this time.

It amused him to hear from the examining physician that he would be admitted under the diagnosis of *severe anxiety/depression syndrome*.

"That way it won't reflect badly against your record," the doctor told him.

Cover up again. Nobody seemed to openly recognize the disease for what it is. Little wonder limited progress is made with this back door approach.

It looked like the company tried to protect itself as well. Bill had always heard the phrase that *God protects old ladies, little children, and drunks.* Perhaps this hospital trip wouldn't be as threatening as he had feared. One of his colleagues, finishing his final week in the ward when Bill entered, quickly gave him an update on how to act and what to say, so that things would go easier.

The results of Bill's blood test left much to be desired. Some of his enzyme levels plotted, "off the chart," the nurse explained. He had heard that before in Okinawa. When he inquired what they would do about it, she told him there would be dietary controls, vitamins, and exercise, but that most of the levels would return to normal in a short while simply by being away from the alcohol.

He had a small room to himself initially, and thought that he had been given special treatment, until he found out the real reason a week later. Isolation might have been necessary if he went through some violent withdrawals, and the other patients would be spared witnessing this display. He remembered the ward in the hospital on Okinawa.

After three days, they placed him in a larger room. Patients called this room, "The Swamp," and it provided some of the much needed socializing atmosphere he would find necessary in his treatment. Just being with others overcame the feeling of isolation, although Bill had never thought he had been affected by being alone. It turned out that, later, he would realize camaraderie played a significant role during the entire period of a patient's recovery.

Seventeen other patients, from all walks of life, formed one large therapy group. Most of the sessions were conducted with all the patients seated in a large circle led by two or three counselors. In the center of the circle, a swivel chair became the "hot seat" upon which each patient would take his or her turn at the proper time, that time when each person reached the fifth week, and neared treatment completion. All the results of their training progress would have been analyzed by then, and this would be the final conditioning for patients prior to release.

It also afforded time for all the other patients to question, and critique the one unlucky enough to be in the chair. Unlucky was the correct word, since these sessions drew down on some pretty deep stuff within the occupant's makeup. Usually gut-wrenching admissions surfaced of all the bad things that had been going on over the years while the person still harbored an addiction to his or her drug of choice. Bill wondered how the counselors could come up with such deeply probing penetrations of the patient's history.

Other training was provided: All patients had to do their own washing and ironing. While difficult for many, Bill's military background allowed him to easily adapt to this situation.

Treatment required a considerable amount of study and homework. The patients had to write on paper many of the feelings, and doubts or desires, that all of them had, not only about their recovery, but also about their past. He thought this to be in keeping with something he had heard about Dr. Sigmund Freud. Physicians and surgeons had devised ways of fixing diseases, and injuries through a hole, which they surgically made in the patient's body. This man, Freud, sometimes called the Father of Psychotherapy, had developed a technique whereby he could see into people's minds by way of a hole in their head. This hole being the mouth, and as patients talked, information about their mental condition would be disclosed. Here, the patients talked about things they had written down.

But human's, even recovering addicts, are a devious lot, and some patients applied an enormous effort to evade the treatment. They only listened to things that they really wanted to hear. Most of them faked their treatment responses. Bill's colleague had quietly told him that after his release, he would play the sobriety game for a short time, then go back to some carefully controlled drinking, being ever so cautious not to be discovered this time. All this to be based on "What I have learned while in this minimum security prison," he had said.

Bill had visits from his family on the allotted days, and they also attended several meetings of their own, without his presence, in order to condition the entire family to the problems which would eventually come after his release, and as the ongoing recovery continued. Bill noticed that most of the other patients had visits from a member, or members of their companies. He felt slighted that no one from his company came to see him. Perhaps they didn't care if he made it or not. This belief left him with a greater level of hostility than he originally thought he had prior to coming into the program.

One day a new patient arrived. He wore the clothes of a cowboy, complete with spurs on his boots. Totally passed out, they put him into the bed next to Bill. He stayed passed out for two more days, then started to look more like he would make it. Bill had never seen anyone so bitter before in his life. This person felt he did not have to be in this recovery center, yet suffered a fit on his fourth day, and had to be restrained by some of the staff to keep from hurting himself. He fought the program for more than a week, then on the second Sunday, raised so much cane, that the staff allowed him to be released in the custody of a friend, in order to attend church. The hospital never saw him again.

Bill had anticipated receiving more from this recovery attempt than his earlier attempt, and he had not been disappointed. In 28 days, the patients went through the entire Big Book, the Twelve Steps, and the Twelve Traditions, plus various amounts of instruction in spirituality, morality, and adapting to a new way of life of sobriety. At times he felt as if they shot machine guns at him. He had a suitcase full of notes. He enjoyed a doctor's presentation on how alcohol affects a person's liver and brain. This science of Biology he could relate to.

All patients received special menus, since most of them required supplemental diets to help regain their health. Bill found that his only restriction had been salt, and he gorged himself. Six days in a row he ordered, and received, steak and lobster for supper.

Bill had been promised physical training by the nurse upon his admission, but nothing of the sort happened. He had been put on a salt-free diet, been given the vitamins, but no exercise program. On his own, Bill ran laps around the hospital parking lot during his free time. He wanted his good health back. He now had a greater resolve to have this program work for him than he did with his previous attempt. He suspected that he would be under close scrutiny once released.

The first two hours of each week day consisted of doctors' and nurses' time. All medications issued, forms filled out, temperature, weight, blood pressure, and similar hospital-related functions transpired. Then it would be the circle, and therapy for the rest of the day, interrupted only by lunch. In the evenings, they would be driven to various AA and NA meetings, depending on the patient's requirements. On the weekends, they had more time to themselves, but still kept busy.

Patients would come up with some of the damndest excuses to try and get out of their required therapy. One girl convinced the staff she needed special gymnastic exercises for her sore back. They allowed her access to the hospital's gymnasium. She told Bill she didn't do any special exercises there, but it was on the other side of the hospital, and she missed an hour of therapy by going there.

Another patient hadn't taken any of his medication in two weeks. A routine inspection found bottles of pills in his locker. He said he was saving them for when he was released. He didn't have a car, and knew he couldn't get to the hospital regularly to pick up his prescriptions.

At no time were patients made to feel they were kept under any type of restraint. In the evenings, on the way to and from outside meetings, each bus or van made stops at a convenience store along the way for health and comfort items. But still, the patients looked for ways to beat the system.

SCHL

One very pretty young girl, a stewardess, confessed to one of
the counselors that he reminded her very much of her father. She
did well with her program, finished treatment early, and with a
minimum of hassling. Bill saw them both chasing around in a
supermarket parking lot three months after his own release. She
looked pregnant, both appeared to be very drunk.

Two days prior to his own turn in the "hot seat" they gave him
a form to fill out which delved very deeply into his personal history.

So this is how they obtained such personal information about us.

On his own hot-seat day, the counselors made a great effort
out of the fact that one of his children had died unexpectedly at
the young age of twenty. He and the rest of the family had been in
the country of Jordan when that sad event had happened, and he
failed to see how this would, or could have anything to do with his
future recovery. Finally, he decided that they called on this strat-
egy to make him feel sad, and to cry in front of the other patients.
He cried. Later, during his third recovery attempt, he would discover, and realize that it is OK for men to cry. But that came later.

As anticipated, his hunch about close scrutiny had been correct. After his release, his employers watched him like a hawk.
Again they put it nicely, though. "We really don't have anything
overseas just now, so we'll use you around here writing lesson plans,
and teaching the more difficult subjects until something breaks,"
he was told. They seemed to still have their faith in his technical
and teaching abilities. He did notice they observed him, albeit
casually, about twice an hour at first.

He went at his recovery effort big time. He joined what he had
been told in the hospital to be the best AA fellowship in the area,
obtained a sponsor, and went to the recommended ninety meetings in the first ninety days. Thereafter, he attended meetings on a
regular basis. For a year he behaved as pure as driven snow, and it
paid off.

"We think you're doing a super job, and we have a nice position for you in Taiwan," they said.

What would be the first thing packed into his briefcase? He put in a fifth of Johnny Walker Red. Not for himself, he said aloud, just in case any of his colleagues over there had a requirement for some scotch. Taiwan is not a dry country, he knew this, and three days after arriving began drinking again in his room. Nine years later he would politely be given an early retirement.

3

Tunnel's End

For some reason, retirement to his planned paradise hadn't worked out for Bill S. He had retired from two relatively successful careers, but still carried around his neck, the stone bottle filled with alcohol, a condition which eventually brought him into a period of extreme loneliness. There didn't seem to be any point at all to all this depression. This feeling became exacerbated by the six by eight foot concrete room, with the iron bed, and the solid steel door he found himself in one night. He had never felt such complete isolation, and the next morning welcomed the judge's direction that he seek treatment for alcohol abuse. Anything to get out of that cell.

Bless people who had, by now, recognized alcoholism as a disease, and tried to make appropriate treatment available. Cost still was an overriding factor for civilians, but for retired military personnel, the Veterans Administration helped people needing care, particularly with Post Traumatic Stress Disorder, PTSD, and mental health problems such as alcoholism.

Early one morning, he presented himself at a dilapidated, though refurbished, yellow prefab building bearing the sign, Veteran's Administration Substance Abuse Treatment (VASAT). He would spend more than a year associated with the recovery personnel working within this building.

He introduced himself to the social worker at the front desk by saying, "I'm in need of treatment for alcohol abuse, I'm told that I can get help here through the VA."

"That is correct," the social worker answered. "Why don't we get you to fill out some forms? We'll begin your admittance and program of treatment right now."

Familiar with paperwork, he filled out the forms, and in short order Bill S found himself seated in a room on a chair with some twenty-odd patients all arranged in a circle. This geometric form would become a permanent member of his soon-to-be-experienced recovery program.

During admission, he had been seen by medical doctors, psychologists, psychiatrists, nurses who drew blood and collected urine, social workers, and therapy specialists. There existed no sham here, he would receive therapy for alcohol abuse, not an anxiety/ depression syndrome.

For four months, mostly seated in the circle, he read the presented literature, did the paperwork assignments, viewed the tapes, vocally contributed to the discussions, and played all the rules of the game. At the end of four months he still hadn't found the magic word, phrase, or technique that would guarantee his successful recovery. The fact that he disregarded everything they told him, almost as promptly as he heard it, never entered his mind as perhaps being one reason why he didn't seem to feel he had made any progress. He still wanted to drive the bus.

During one of his sessions, a new female patient spoke with words that caught his attention. This patient had just come from six weeks of treatment in a residential center. She spoke words that sounded to him like wisdom he hadn't been made aware of in all his past treatment attempts. Up until this time, Bill had been an out-patient, living at home, and attending classes and sessions at the VASAT during the day. He decided that in order to get anywhere with his recovery treatment, he had to be admitted to this in-patient center.

The building could be seen from the yellow prefab, a three-story monstrosity, fenced at one end, and with bars around all the windows. The place appeared foreboding, but he wanted to try if it meant he could get on with his recovery. This was the old "Psych" building where mental patients had been treated.

He spoke at great length to the new patient, interested in not only what she had to say, but also how she said it. She presented a confidence with her approach that he hadn't detected in any of the other patients. Neither he nor the woman smoked, and during the scheduled smoking breaks, they would retire to a small gazebo on a lot across the street, and talk. She did most of the talking. She told her story of attempted recovery failures, very similar to his own, and how this residential approach had been the trigger that had provided her with the recovery program she worked on now.

During a break in his training, he walked up to the three-story building, and struck up a conversation with one of the psychologists. They would be glad to have him. Next, he spoke with his counselor about being transferred. No problem there.

Several weeks later, he walked into the Residential Recovery Center with all the proper paperwork needed. However, his thoughts still included the approach he expected his recovery to take. All the people he initially met, seemed cordial and glad to see him, and it surprised him to find that his living quarters were barracks–no big deal after all the time he had spent in the Marines. Unknown at the time, this living arrangement, with its attendant back porch atmosphere, would provide him with the proper recovery information to save his life.

They kept him busy, but also allotted time for personal things. He spent most of his free time at the gym or running around the track. Five nights a week the patients would be bused to outside AA meetings. Monday night they cleaned up their quarters and the public rooms of the center, and on Sundays, the center hosted patients from other recovery facilities on their huge patio.

Barbeque, a big event, took second place to volleyball. Sometimes the games would go on into the small hours of the morning. An enormous amount of energy, in the form of hostility and frustration, could be released by the games, and other events that transpired in and around this patio. Some patients even bought a small, eight-foot, children's plastic swimming pool at the PX that received constant use, even at night, although one could only sit in the foot-deep water.

This small attempt at a family atmosphere helped, and contributed immensely to everyone's recovery attitude. He had raised four children, but something started coming through here that he missed from his own background. Other patients admitted they felt the same. Being sober helped.

To teach him humility, he had been assigned kitchen police. This had been done, not by the staff, but by senior patients who made up the leadership element of the community of patients. They had been in similar situations earlier in their treatment, and he would be placed in a like position later. Kitchen police didn't bother him, and he felt good whenever he received compliments that the kitchen hadn't looked this clean in a long while.

Still, for the next two and one-half weeks he disregarded anything they told him that he didn't want to hear. Then something remarkable happened to him during the third week. He would openly admit later that what happened had been his turning point. That time, and he couldn't pinpoint it exactly, revealed to him, he felt, when he had hit his bottom. From that time forward, he began asking for help, and listening to what others had to say. He started to *want* to recover, he started to *want* to get better.

To help him to get a better understanding of spirituality, he volunteered to be the Spiritual Leader during the latter portion of his treatment. Each morning, the community held its own role call, did all the administrative things for starting the day and future planning, and began with a spiritual reading for the day.

One day he received a compliment from a female patient with tears in her eyes. She thanked him for his reading. Somewhat embarrassed, he said that he hadn't created those words, just read them. She told him she knew that, it was for the way he had read them that she thanked him. For him, this was scary. His words could make others cry.

A little at a time he became aware of the small ways in which other people were helping each other, something he hadn't felt he needed most of his life.

Spirituality became an inviting word after he began to understand it. It invited him to discover a new world of values and beliefs. He began to develop a new lifestyle as things important to him began to change. He took himself out of the driver's seat. Spirituality provided a new basis for all his decisions and relationships. Yet, it didn't come easy, it required work. It had to be conducted against a natural inclination to keep things the same, never changing–to cling to his old way of doing things. He had to extend himself, make totally free choices, not acts of conformity, living one day at a time. He learned to seek and try new ideas, looked for a new way of life, one significantly better-structured to seeking out goodness, joy, sobriety, truth, love, and spirituality.

Looking outward in his search for new directions, he became able to go beyond his former, limited space, and begin exploring new and fresh ideas, possibilities, and alternatives. He began not only to look at himself differently, he also went through an important change in how he felt about himself.

For a while, he felt like three separate persons: He appeared as one person to other people, he had an idea about how he appeared to himself, and then the most fascinating part of it, he began to discover who he really could be. He had arrived at a time in his recovery when he met a perfect stranger. He became blessed with an ability to recognize his real self, and an even greater realization of what and whom he could become. Each positive day of his recovery, he got to know more and more about the perfect stranger whom he had met only recently. It presented a glorious feeling for him to know this person.

He also became aware of a process he called healing in action. He thought it to be one of the most beautiful things he could see and experience. He saw other recovering people, and their appearance advertised how their programs progressed. Success shone from them like a light. To him, healing meant offering gratitude. He healed himself by being thankful, it would become one of the reasons that he would continue going to meetings. As he healed, he felt that he told a story. When he saw others sober and recovering, he, in turn, received a healing benefit from them. It's easy to change the story. It is something like a self-rejuvenating book–the cover changes along with the words inside. He took from life every day, it became only natural for him that he give something back. He called it payback.

He began acquainting himself with positive affirmations, simple words or phrases that he repeated to himself whenever he felt a funk, a state of paralyzed fear, coming on. He knew that when his mind became stressed out, his body would be prone to make mistakes. Whenever he felt that he became troubled, he tried to stop, take a breath, and refocus. He thought other thoughts that were oriented around positive ideas. He learned to meditate. Meditation allowed him to acquire mental images that became soothing and relaxing. Meditation acted as a mental massage, putting positive attitudes into his mind, and therefore, his mood.

His whole attitude began changing. It became important for him not only to have the right ideas about recovery, but also the right motives. Getting sober is not recovery, it is only a discovery, or perhaps a rediscovery of the things wrong with him. It is the beginning of a more gradual approach at the healing process that will allow him to experience peace, not conflict, and to be in touch with something higher than himself. He began living his sobriety on a daily basis, he couldn't borrow it from others, he had to earn it, one step at a time by himself, and it took an effort on his part. He realized that his recovery would take him the rest of his life.

Each night, the patients gathered on the porch adjacent to the barracks he lived in. Many patients in this barracks were elderly, and the younger ones came to look to them as being wiser, because of their age. At first this pleased him, and then he found out that the age for a recovering person was not how many years that person had lived, but how many years that person had lived sober.

Wisdom came with the length of time a person's recovery program had been practiced, and from the amount of improvement realized. There is no definite pace at which this occurs. It is strictly up to each individual as to how much, and how fast, things can be taken in and digested. One of his most significant realizations had come from a young woman slightly over the age of sixteen.

The young girl had made him realize that he had been fighting his program, trying to maintain his control, when what needed to happen would be for him to open up, let things begin happening to him, and "sort of roll with the punches", as she had explained.

From this time on, he began listening to what others had to say. He noticed the effects their words had on their own programs, and then began taking in and using bits and pieces of everything he heard. He molded them into what would eventually become his own personal recovery program. A program that he realized would have to be flexible enough to constantly change, if he were to get anywhere with it. Wanting recovery was his key to turning things around.

Bill S began to afford himself the luxury of again looking forward to making plans. He always had been a day dreamer, but became so terribly disappointed whenever his better laid plans failed, that he had developed a failure-prior-to-investigation attitude. Typical of most addicts, this is a most difficult attitude to overcome. It is all right to make plans, and to dream of better things. The trick is to not let oneself become too wrapped up in great expectations, leaving room for change when some of the dreams don't, or can't happen.

There is a four-letter word for fertilizer. Bill had been convinced that for most of his life he had been destined to wander about in it over his head. From time to time he might become brave enough to stir things up a bit, but he never managed to change much. Eventually, his life would be relegated back to the restricting canopy of the overhanging fertilizer. The chaplain came to his rescue.

He reminded Bill that a seed, when planted, is usually covered with fertilizer. Undaunted, the seed accepts this predicament, and begins to grow up and out to the light.

It didn't dawn on Bill that until he had spoken, and listened to the young woman, that he could also rise above it. He could plant his feet firmly in the ground as his head rose high.

BOOK TWO

4

Patient X   The Waffling Politician

Patient X is the waffling politician, who presented a flamboyant attitude, and an outgoing presence. A retired major, he had arrived two days late for his scheduled admission, and gave the lame excuse that his motorcycle had broken down. Most active duty patients admitted to a recovery center arrive by Military Airlift Command flights, helicopter, or are provided ground transportation, depending upon their individual work situations, duty stations, and travel distances involved. There is something to be said for this supervised, or controlled transportation, at least it is timely. Retired patients are left to their own transportation devices.

Patient X related a history fraught with blackouts: Periods during which a person functioned unconsciously, not being able to recall anything that had happened. He spoke of riding the entire distance from Eureka to San Diego, California, and not remembering anything. He showed receipts of motels along the route, and a tour guide from Big Sur National Park. He steadfastly maintained that he could not recall anything that had happened during the trip. He had blocked out three complete days of his life. His group-mates would come upon him in the evenings, as he contemplated the receipts and the tour guide, in a futile attempt to regain some recollection of the lost time.

He possessed a highly imaginative intelligence which he demonstrated in various ways. He appeared well educated, voluble, and an avid prankster. His favorite pastime had him searching through magazines for cartoons whose action indicated something familiar to the proffered treatment of all the patients. He would erase the printed words, and substitute words of his own that would be hilarious, yet right on target to most of the treatment objectives. He taped all of these cartoons on the door of the Chief Psychologist's office.

He admitted to having attended several recovery centers while on active duty, and came to this latest one by way of VA referral. His memory was eidetic, or he had kept all his previous recovery notes and lessons. His participation at all his counseling sessions saw him divulge textbook answers. But, he would get some of them twisted. For example, he would say, "I know I'll feel better soon if I can just make you feel better." This exhibited an unhealthy reliance on the control of exterior things in order to fulfill his own interior needs.

Another favorite saying of his, "I sure hope my past gets better soon so I can get on with building my future." Here, being hung up in the past prevents any work in the present, and for any future improvement.

He constantly gave advice on how to recover to everyone he encountered. He understood everybody's problems, and exactly how they could be cured. It became embarrassing sometimes. In AA meetings, when a fellowship member related encountering difficulty dealing with a personal problem, he would seek that person out after the meeting, and offer his solution.

"I can tell you exactly how to handle this problem," he would say, "we discussed that very same subject several days ago in one of our counseling sessions. This is what you must do. . ." Then he would proceed to inform the listener about his own recommended solution to the problem. The person, usually having many years of sobriety, would smile slightly, thank him for his efforts, and go about his or her way.

It would be extremely difficult to pin Patient X down to any specific item within his own recovery program. He always seemed to be working on whatever topic appeared to be current at the moment. It became apparent to all who associated with him, that he never heeded his own advice.

His compelling outlook had *religion* simply being an organized system of faith and worship, while *spirituality* existed as a vital principle in living things, giving rise to animation. He saw a distinct separation between the two, neither one necessary for a successful recovery program, and this severely curtailed his spiritual progress.

He steadfastly refused to use the tools that his counselors presented, therefore the process of learning, and understanding his new recovery program never got off the ground. His mental efforts stayed somewhere between unconscious incompetence, that is, not knowing what he did, and conscious incompetence, not being aware of what he should do. He never practiced to attain his conscious competence level, thereby allowing further progress to the final level of unconscious competence, where he would be able to do things right without having to think about them. Most of the other patients felt his time in recovery to be simply wasted.

He spent all his time wrapped up in a totally subjective approach to analyze himself. He never tried to take a few symbolic steps away, and to see himself objectively. He constantly risked losing his private war, by staying overly-engrossed in some small fire fight.

There are generally four basic reasons most people familiar with recovery therapy will accept as contributing to a person's addiction: One is genetic inheritance, over which the person has little or no control, the second and third deal with environmental and peer pressures creating stress, and the fourth is simply that the person abuses the use of his or her drug of choice, in a never-ending pursuit of continuing gratification. This final reason is perhaps the most common, and Patient X put the sole blame of his problem on his inability to *physically* handle alcohol. He never accepted that his mental attitude may have contributed.

Most addictions begin when people start experimenting with alcohol, and continues when they find that it reduces their inhibitions, thereby providing feelings of relaxation. Their social status seems to improve, and they like the anticipation of the next period of use. Group participation, or drinking in populated bars, is a common way to begin. A kind of pseudo-sociability is felt that offers comfort for many who are lonely, and who have difficulty seeking and acquiring friends. However, a more dangerous path usually follows, where the drinking person begins seeking stimulation from the alcohol in an otherwise boring environment. This is a danger on military posts, and is extremely popular in most living quarters provided to single servicemen, particularly officers.

Patient X had used alcohol as a magnet to attract people to him. As his confidence elevated because of his increased consumption, he would attempt to persuade his audience to accept his own outlooks and opinions. By doing this, he felt he would be providing a service, not only to others, but to himself as well.

As with all addicts, he never became aware of the point in time, when his consumption ceased being voluntary, and began escalating, finally becoming uncontrollable. Drinking on weekends, or bi-weekly gatherings, quickly condensed into nightly affairs, and ultimately included all day as well as most of the night. He became motivated by his desire to attain a specific effect from his drinking, rather than using it only for circumstantial or situational incidents. In other words, he drank to get drunk. His addiction had arrived.

Patient X freely shared his own excuses with those around him. He constantly related how his increased consumption of alcohol had become a necessary way of life throughout his military career. Each promotion had been an excuse to drink while he had been enlisted, and this continued after he had achieved officer status. In fact, each time he had not been promoted also contributed a reason to get drunk. For other excuses he used Staff NCO functions, bosses nights, mess nights, and monthly functions at the officer's club, wherein each unit on the base would have its own opportunity to outdo the previous host-battalion in extent and scope. He spoke of being in one unit where the commanding officer required any officer, not a member of the club, to write a personal letter stating his reasons why. Most junior officers, fearing nonmembership would reflect badly on their records, joined. It became customary to drink lunch at the club, and to attend the happy hour immediately after work each day.

Patient X had two very distinct beliefs that he tried to force onto others. He believed, that every person had the individual right, to do things his or her way, in order to ensure success. The other belief, the one he voiced constantly, stated that each person had a given right to worry. Worrying made for the fundamental starting point of correcting all wrongs, but for him, worrying brought about constant feelings of anger. He justified this, by saying that if he stayed angry all the time, and at everyone, then nobody could sneak up and surprise him, with something that would hurt him. He felt that he could never be hurt, as long as he remained suspicious of everyone else. Consequently, he worried a lot, and his anger never left him.

Anger is a feeling like happiness, but anger is a strong displeasure. It can be a very strong emotion, and usually covers up other feelings like guilt, fear, and hurt. Approached wrongly, anger can endanger recovery. If properly understood, it can enhance self-knowledge and serenity. While Patient X carried his anger around with him always, he constantly remained on guard to avoid any expression that even suggested anger. Consequently, his pent-up anger became cold and resentful. By keeping his cold anger inside, it added to his level of worrying. Trapped in this self-feeding circle, his anger eventually would burst forth, and be released with words or actions that ended up causing pain to others. Throughout his entire stay in therapy, he missed the point that patience and good temper are required if any successful program is to be adopted.

For Patient X, his fear of going back into the real world presented an insurmountable challenge. Literally terrified, but unwilling to admit this fact, he vacillated. His release would have occurred on the usual last day of his sixth week, although this particular Friday marked the beginning of a five-day holiday for the military. Patient X talked the recovery center into allowing him to remain in the barracks for the additional five days, under the guise that he didn't wish to travel over the highways during the holiday.

He spent the five days as if he were still a patient. He continued to attend the AA meetings, in itself a good sign, but refused to discuss anything, remaining resolute and cold at all times. He entered into no conversation whatsoever, and appeared to be in a visible fright. At various times, he would mount his cycle, drive slowly around the streets surrounding the center, as if practicing or attempting to mind set himself for the forthcoming trip. In this way, he built up false courage, this time without alcohol, and most of the patients suspected it would only be a short time before he would go back to drinking.

After the holiday, he hung around an additional two days, finally leaving on the morning of the eighth day. He had promised to send post cards from each of his stops, on his trip back to Mississippi, but nobody ever received any. The people in the center never heard from him.

5

Patient Y The Comic Relief Artist

To Patient Y, the Comic Relief Artist, life, as well as her recovery, appeared to be a joke. She talked loud, and did and said everything with an air of lightness, and comedic retinues–she took nothing seriously. In the beginning, denial of her addiction manifested itself in laughter.

Take, for instance, her initial impression of the construction of her Time Line. A Time Line is a graph, that illustrates quantity of consumption, over the years, of a patient's selected drugs of choice. Like any graph, it talks to people who read it, indicating among other things, just where in a person's life uncontrolled consumption begins. At first, it is difficult to begin construction of a Time Line, but gradually, as the history is put down on paper, memory is able to divulge incidents long forgotten, and eventually, when worked on diligently, the Time Line takes shape. Colored entries make entering and reading information easier.

Patient Y's initial comments concerning her Time Line came in a highly irresponsible manner.

"I tried to get them to allow me to finish only the first and last pages," she said, "and that all the other pages in between could be covered by one huge blackout–13 years' long. They didn't buy it."

On the left side of her Time Line, things began innocently enough, as her consumption had begun gradually. As entries progressed to the right, substance quantities increased, punctuated by significant events causing dips, but usually spikes along the overall slope of the incline.

Collectively, every other patient's Time Line also showed huge increases in consumption, as his or her chart advanced. Addiction is a progressive disease, as long as we continue to drink and use, we only get worse, never better.

It dawned on her that certain environmental, and peer pressure-related incidents, had had significant influence on her overall consumption. She could see those places and times in her past, where she had been running from reality, avoiding responsibility, and taking the easy way out as she studied her documented information. Some entries jumped out at her, in nasty realizations, which would have a redeeming effect on her recovery program once she began living it.

The entire world exists as a society, and as such, begins to develop certain societal characteristics. One such characteristic is a behavior similar to what a flock of birds or a school of fish exhibits. It is a type of mob-psychology where everyone behaves as an integrated unit.

In our modern-day, world-society, we are fear oriented. We have a great fear of the unknown, and the first reaction most people have when confronted by this unknown fear is to destroy it. Another typical reaction is to run away.

Our bodies develop weapons for these defenses. We become frustrated and hostile at the very least. Running from our fears is probably the single most significant reason that people begin drinking and using, eventually becoming addicted–a security blanket is made available that covers our basic expectation of danger.

In recovery, after detoxification, the patient is all too aware that the security blanket has been taken away. The body feels strange, has difficulty accepting this new feeling of anxiety, and needs some reassurance that things aren't as bad as they seem.

Part of the recovery syndrome for all new patients includes loud talking. Every new patient does it, and when asked why, usually is unaware of the fact, and it gradually goes away in several weeks. Loud talking is a defense mechanism against fear, called up to convince the patient that whatever it is that he or she is involved with at the moment is the right thing to do, the comforting thing. It is an unconscious reaction, and as I said, usually goes away in a few weeks.

Some of the older patients, here the term "older" refers to those patients nearing completion of their own treatment, use the passage of loud talking as an indication in the new patients that recovery progress is beginning to take hold.

Patient Y always carried a stack of three-by-five cards with her, fanned out, which she would wave in front of her face whenever she felt a certain subject needed to be punctuated with some levity.

The cards had been assigned by her counselor as ongoing exercises to help analyze shortcomings and defects of character in Patient Y's overall behavior. At the top of each card she had to write an emotion or feeling. Then she filled in the rest of the card with explanations and justifications why this emotion had either positive or negative effects, and how it related to her overall recovery. Some patients had stacks of cards four and five inches thick by the time they finished their stay at the recovery center.

"I dee-clare," she would say in a mock southern accent, and wave her cards. "This li'l ol' therapeutic program has me in a terrible tizzy. I do believe they're tryin' to compromise me."

Another therapeutic approach, that suffered her clownish ridicule, was an exercise in anger control. Patients had been given a drawing of a thermometer, in the center of a blank page. The task required that each person fill in all emotions, and feelings, that might register symbolically on this thermometer, as danger signals associated with rage. Those words at the top of the drawing, would have more significance than those at the bottom, and more time would be spent analyzing these for corrective actions to reduce their effects.

Patient Y crowded all her entries near the top of the drawing, changed the picture to indicate the top of the thermometer exploding, and spewing out the colored fluid in a fountain effect. She never admitted if she really felt this way about all her emotions, but most other patients assumed, if she modified her drawing in this fashion, she inwardly possessed such feelings, and that they had significant effects on her. It served as a lesson in reality to other patients, to see this type of approach. Some of the patients, I had occasion to see in the years following my own release, still worked on a daily basis trying to overcome, or at least reduce, effects of long-term, pent-up anger. It is a giant emotion having huge impetus with addicts.

During an exercise in spirituality, she showed her group an approach that she had adopted with her search for a Higher Power. She boldly told everyone that she had written a want ad. It read as follows:

> *Wanted, one Higher Power. Applicant must be kind and loving, not judgmental or critical. Must work for zero wages, but be available anytime during the day or night. Must possess boundless energy, stamina, and imagination as well as unfailing courage. Must be adaptable to operating in various types of environments, both comfortable and foreboding. Must be able to issue challenges, encourage the healthy release of emotions, and be able to help me unleash my creative expressions. Above all, must be extremely patient. Applicant need not apply in person.*

"I didn't have the courage to send it to the newspaper," she said. "I thought someone might answer. Then I wouldn't know how to handle that."

The chaplain had made a comment to the effect that, while on the face of it, the submission of a want ad to a newspaper, might at first seem facetious, that it really demonstrated an inherent desire to search for, and find, the concept behind a Higher Power. Like the newspaper article published to answer Virginia's question asking if Santa Claus is real, this approach is sincere in its quest, and provides a solid foundation from which to begin formulating a Higher Power concept. He distributed copies to everyone in his other classes, since "the job description came right to the point."

As the weeks progressed, a visible change could be seen taking place in Patient Y. She stopped feeling unworthy, felt less disgraced, and gradually regained some of her lost self respect. Others could see develop a slow transition from funny to serious. Patient Y attained some humility, lost her hostility, and no longer seemed afraid to ask for help. From her three-by-five cards, the two emotions, shame and guilt surfaced, and she managed to reverse their effects, to turn around some of her remorse at having embarrassed parts of her life, although she still joked about everything.

Then, because of something within her makeup, Patient Y suddenly changed her entire outlook. The other patients noticed almost at the exact moment that it occurred: She made up her mind that she *wanted* to recover. To all patients in treatment for alcohol, and other drug abuse, this is a critical realization, and for most becomes the turning point for them. They want to get better, and they do, even if it is only slowly at first.

If there is a redeeming word in this confusing world of recovery, a driving word causing an unrelenting desire to refrain from the old way, and to seek new things, free from the effects of drugs, that word is *want*. If a patient wants to recover, his or her chances for recovery are excellent. If the patient does not want to recover, all the exposure to any amount of therapy will not work. Recovery requires a tremendous effort from the sick person, it is not an easy task at first, and requires work. Indeed, the task of recovering requires that the person remain on constant alert for signs that will cause relapses, to notice these signs, and to take certain steps to counter impulses so that return to drug addiction does not occur. Something as simple as verbally admitting, "I am alcoholic", as ineffectual as this may seem, serves as an audible reminder of the problem, and reinforces a person's determination to stay clean.

In a passionate outburst, Patient Y shared her experience with all of us, when she admitted that she had experienced realization as to what Step One meant to her. This is a very critical point in anyone's recovery, and for some becomes quite emotional.

In Step One, we admit that there is a problem. For Patient Y, she also did a few other things during the experience of living through her realization of Step One. She related that she became aware, she surrendered, she became honest, and above all, she *accepted* the simple fact that she suffered from the disease of alcoholism.

To her, this became a revelation. **She was alcoholic.** Now she could knuckle down and begin to do something about it. Now she could get on her way to working at a program of recovery that would restore her lost self respect. She felt she could use the Twelve Steps as a guide to keep things in order, to help her along the way. She said that with some help from others she could do it, that she wanted to do it.

As she neared the time for her release from the program, she also related how she felt with the next two steps. These steps are the spiritual discoveries that most patients feel are so necessary to further the solid foundation required for progress in recovery.

She disclosed her feelings on how she interpreted steps two and three.

In Step Two I became comfortable with the feeling that I am no longer completely in control of my life. I accept that something external to myself is there to aid and assist in my recovery program. Serenity is the fallout, once I understand, that with my new outlook, I need never be alone again. I have faith in something that I don't fully understand, and I'm ok with that feeling. Some of us refer to this external source of newfound energy as a Higher Power. To some, it's the power of the group. For others, it's simply realizing something else is there. To me it is a God of my understanding.

In Step Three, once realizing that there is something else out there to help, I had to be willing to turn my problems over. Now I can have relief from my problems. Immediate solutions are no longer a big requirement, sometimes simply waiting a while will solve some of them. Sometimes they are of my own mental creation, not real at all, and simply will go away as my mind clears. I had to release my egocentric control, and simply turn my problems over to this external source of energy that is there to help. I realize, by using the power inherent within the first three steps, that I can find assistance in discovering, and solving, the requirements of the remaining nine steps.

Her smile still remained throughout each remaining day, and the jokes still came, although fewer and less often. To the other patients, who continually noticed her progress, she served as a sparkling reminder that people can recover, and they can get better from the effects of alcohol.

I last saw her at a birthday meeting. She received her nine-year token. She told me that during the first year of her recovery, she hadn't stopped after completing the recommended ninety meetings in ninety days. She said that she had attended something like 500 meetings during that first year. She had missed so much while drinking that she now had her sights set on rediscovering all the things she had denied herself in the past. She said that she still went to meetings, spoke to her sponsor regularly, and that she tried to live each day to its fullest potential, trying to make the best of all situations, even if they might be negative.

Seeing her renewed my faith in my own recovery.

6

Patient Z The Grumpy Curmudgeon

Patient Z is the Grumpy Curmudgeon. He has attempted recovery many times, yet remains set in his ways. Nobody else's ideas are right for him since they've never seemed to work.

This patient's military career goes back to the early days of the Korean Conflict. In those days, reaction from his training had been unalterable: If the guy on the other side didn't respond correctly, one simply killed him. This attitude may be acceptable while on the battle fields of war, but Patient Z continues to maintain this outlook long after the hostilities have ceased. His predator mind set still remains, even though his contract with his former military commitment has stopped. Now he fights the battle within himself, and not being able to respond with deadly force, won't kill himself outright, but doesn't know how to keep from killing himself slowly with alcohol. That he needs to change his overall outlook on survival in no way seeps through his mental conditioning. He is unable to heal since he doesn't want to.

Constantly violating the HALT Rule, he's lost in a sea of memories that he can't lose. He continually stays *Hungry*, not just for food, but also for his drug of choice, alcohol. He's *Angry* always. Angry with others since he feels most, if not all, of his problems are their fault, and angry with himself since he can't solve this current problem with something as simple as a bullet. Consequently, he remains *Lonely* and *Tired*. He can be lonely in a room full of people, which is why he avoids others as much as possible. He's tired all the time from the efforts spent at avoidance, constant worry, an interminable amount of complaining, and constantly wondering where his next drink is, so that he can escape into the never-never-land of make-believe–a place he visits more often as his condition worsens. PTSD, or Post Traumatic Stress Disorder, is no doubt a contributing factor now, but is not to be blamed for his alcoholism. Proper treatment, and understanding of his own weaknesses, are probably two of the things he should be trying to filter out from his recovery attempts, but he isn't seeing anything beyond old memories. His current residential stay will result in a brief period of sobriety, simply a dry drunk, and he will resume drinking soon after he leaves. He churlishly covets life as he remembers it from long ago, although his impressions have changed considerably over the years, from damage to his brain and his memory faculties, of which he is unaware.

There is a "dip stick" comparison that can be used to explain his condition. We are all familiar with the dip stick that measures the level of oil in automotive engines. There is a cross-hatched space near the bottom of the stick, within which the oil level should remain if engine operation is to continue correctly, and the appearance of the oil should be clean. The human body and brain can be equated to a similar approach, in measuring proper operating levels, which bio-medical people call homeostasis. In the balance of keeping the body and brain running correctly, a symbolic dipstick, thrust inside, should indicate within the acceptable area of tolerance, or things start going awry. Patient Z's physiological dip stick reading would indicate well away from the safe area, and the appearance of blood and neurotransmitters would appear very cloudy. A significant imbalance is present, and a symbolic "oil change" is necessary. This is what treatment attempts to provide, but unless the patient is willing to allow the old, dirty stuff, to be replaced with new, clean stuff, no progress is made.

In his earlier years, he prided himself with the rationale that he had always looked at things intellectually. He felt that he had the wisdom to understand things with a minimum of complexity. Now his mental processes are tangled in a snarl of intellectual

presuppositions which usually fail to bring any surcease from his
alcoholic addiction. He stays in an endless litany of moaning or
crying about the old days. He laments the loss of his youthful
vigor, always seeming to be on a pity pot. His mantra of
insufficiency cries, "Poor me, poor me, (pour) me another
drink."

Other patients, trying to talk with him, come away with the
same, universal effect–they all admit coming away with negative
impressions. It seemed almost as if he drew some vital force from
others. "Absorbed something, as if using a sponge," as one patient
stated, which left him feeling depressed or empty. Left unchecked,
these feelings of inadequacy had grown so intense over the years
that they took over his entire psyche.

As his consumption of alcohol increased, pure gratification
resulted temporarily, but each cyclical withdrawal period became
more difficult for Patient Z, finally reaching a point where he found
it easier, if not cheaper, to try and stay partly drunk all of the time.

His personal bout with alcohol began at an early age. He acquired the taste as an innocent enjoyment, which escalated quickly
from social use to compulsive, solitary drinking. Intoxication gave
way to dependency with its psychological and physical debilitation.

He developed a weight problem early in his life–alcohol, and
its mixing elements, especially in the quantities required by heavy
drinkers, contain an enormous number of calories. Couple this
with the lack of a desire for exercise, something else induced by
alcohol consumption, and it becomes difficult for the drinking
person to keep from gaining weight. Along with being overweight,
there are other, more serious conditions.

Of the more severe diseases, liver deterioration is usually the
beginning. At first the organ simply becomes enlarged, as its mo-
lecular structure changes, and its tissues harden. Except for the
skin, the liver is our largest organ. When it enlarges, it can't move
backward, ribs and backbone are in the way, so it naturally pushes
forward. A person's belt doesn't stretch much so the familiar pot

belly, or "beer belly" results. Patient Z probably hadn't seen his own belt buckle, except in a reflection, in many years.

Because his alcoholism has been chronic, degenerative liver disease is present. This degeneration of the liver is known as cirrhosis. Portal cirrhosis is the most prevalent form occurring in alcoholics. The condition is usually irreversible, but supportive treatment sometimes can result in partial regeneration. Treatment consists of diet control, vitamins, diuretics, and beta blockers. Antabuse, (disulfiram) is sometimes given to patients to help prevent relapse, since it induces a terrible reaction against alcohol which causes the patient to believe a heart attack is happening. Naltrexone, effective treatment with narcotics abusers, has recently been used with alcoholics. Along with the psychological counseling, this treatment is given by the medical staff in recovery centers, but makes little headway since more alcohol is consumed after release from treatment, thereby destroying still more liver molecules.

Other organs, like the kidneys and pancreas suffer as well. First come painful attacks of indigestion followed by gallbladder problems. This is followed by severe delirium tremens (a condition characterized by deliriousness, violent trembling, hallucinations, and seizures). As is the usual case, more alcohol, with its numbing effects, is called for, further agitating the disabilities. Sleeping becomes difficult, and again alcohol is called upon–this time to aid in providing a night's rest. Only it isn't sleep that comes, the drinker usually passes out, leaving the body and mind to continue its inadequate purifying chores with the drinker in painless oblivion. Once the damage to the brain and heart becomes severe enough, death is the result.

Patient Z's relapses have followed the time-honored pattern of all alcoholics. His sipping turned to gulping, and in his endless march of personal tragedy, his disease progressed in ever-advancing stages. First came bloodshot and glassy eyes, then it seemed to be poor coordination, escalating to unsteady balance, violent muscular tremors, and finally, occasional hysteria. About this time,

Patient Z usually showed up at a recovery center, in another futile attempt to learn what went wrong this last time.

Learning involves replacing old, automatic, patterns with new ones. This patient doesn't want to learn. His new brain, the cerebral cortex, will never get the chance to begin controlling things within his body and mind. He will forever remain under his old brain's control, receiving little more than the basic survival directions which includes hunger, thirst, and sex. His sexual drive, as well as the other two, however, has been replaced with a desire for intoxication. Therefore, he will regularly suffer relapses. His old mind will continue to look at sobriety as a penance, not a fulfillment. He will continue to get worse, never better.

In one session he related that at one time he had considered himself to be the world's greatest alcoholic. He could drink more, last longer, and recover more quickly than all his previous drinking partners. While he believed this claim for a time, even he admitted that he hadn't been the world's greatest.

"One time I went to a party," he said, "and they told me the bar was free, that I could drink all I wanted. You know, I couldn't do it. My mind said 'go ahead,' but my body said 'whoa.' I passed out"

In spite of this revelation, the craving for alcohol persisted, and overruled any other desire. He spent an alcohol-related two-year term in jail when younger, and this confinement forced him to remain dry for that time. Obviously, healing had to have taken place, but within a year after release, he ended up in worse shape than when he had been incarcerated.

Nationwide statistics show that three out of four recovering addicts will not make it beyond two years. When patients leave any treatment center, there is no way of telling into which category they will fall. A success rate of twenty-five percent isn't very high. How can these odds be increased? One way is to go to meeting places, and surround oneself with many persons who make up the twenty-five percent. These meetings are held all over the country, in all the cities and counties. All a person has to do is look in the yellow pages under A. Not enough people do this though.

"This time when I get out," Patient Z said over and over, "I'm going to do things differently. I owe it to my wife, to my children, and to my grand kids. I know that they will give me a reason for staying sober."

His face lit up, and his movements appeared to be more agile, whenever his family came to visit, but Patient Z overlooked one of the most obvious, yet most difficult rules to drive into a recovering person's mind. A person must want sobriety for his or herself, alone, or it won't work.

All our lives we have been lying to everyone, even ourselves, and attempting to put the cause of our recovery on another. This is *the* lie. Nobody made us get the way we are. We did it ourselves, to ourselves. In like fashion, nobody will make us toe the line, and stay sober. We must do this ourselves, for ourselves. Once sobriety, and a solid recovery program are laid down, the benefits begin happening, to us, as well as others.

Bill sometimes wished that Patient X might have been at the same recovery center with Patient Z. He thought that perhaps the driving intent of X telling Z what he must do might somehow penetrate the defenses of Z's mind.

But he realized that this is not the case. Even if Patient Z listened, it would be strictly up to Patient Z to adopt his own recovery program. Should this, by some miracle happen, and Z took some of X's advice, so much the better, but Patient Z still had to do it for himself. It doesn't work any other way.

On the day Patient Z left, the other patients gave him a small party for encouragement.

"I want to thank each and every one of you for boosting my morale" he said, "and encouraging me to keep sober. I won't let you down."

Bill would have felt better had he heard the words, "I won't let myself down."

BOOK THREE

7

Structure

While most patients will state that they are self-referred into their respective recovery programs, the opposite is usually true. Most patients are referred to treatment via an intervening person or situation—a desperate spouse or family member, a judge, or a commanding officer usually causes the admission. This procedure is called an intervention. The underlying reason, however, is always the same: Admission occurs as a result of a person losing control because of drug abuse, and becoming impaired with the functioning of his or her everyday life.

Many patients are active duty military, and have been referred as a result of one or more drunk driving incidents. Seeing something in the person's basic makeup, supervisors take the chance, and have the person admitted in lieu of disciplinary action. Sometimes, rehabilitated people do not make the unit's punishment record look bad, and this may be the reason, although this is not too often admitted as being the case. Referral does result in turning around a significant number of good men who would otherwise be lost.

Patients are a diverse lot, drugs and alcohol being totally unselective with their choosing. All ranks, from generals on down to the lowest private, active or retired, are represented. Some are from positions of respect and authority: Critically skilled lawyers, anesthesiologists, even surgeons, and these latter individuals, with their medical affiliation, usually have become addicted to self-prescribed, self-administered drugs of a controlled nature. An enormous number of veterans are involved in recovery, some dating back to WWII.

The usual time allotted for therapy, by the latest presidential edict, is three weeks, but one week to as many as six weeks or more can be granted. It all seems to depend on what costs the insurance of the admitting authority will bear. It's extremely unfortunate, but nobody, nowhere, provides free rehabilitation services. Three weeks is hardly long enough for severely addicted patients to detoxify, let alone be expected to have readjusted, learned, and progressed a sufficient distance into a recovery program, to justify releasing them back into society.

A typical military recovery center I attended consisted of the following. The facility had been headed by two separate individuals: One, a recovering military officer in charge of doctors and nursing personnel, and one civilian, in charge of psychologists and counselors. Other staff members consisted of clerical and medical technicians. Military personnel consisted of a three-to-one majority over civilians. Some counselors claimed to be recovering, most did not, relying upon training for their expertise. Usually, therapy groups, called cycles, consisted of no more than eight patients with assigned counselors not exceeding three.

The medical technicians consisted of an unusual lot, mostly female, unmarried with children, pregnant, or both, and just serving time until their enlistments expired, or they had their babies. All of them had been supposedly trained in medical or therapeutic specialty, some in psychiatry, and some in social work. I noticed many basic skills to be lacking. An example: The senior technician, called the Ward Master, on several occasions, could not operate a simple breathalyser.

Almost everyone seemed illiterate when operating computers at even the most basic level. Those select few having any computer expertise at all, seemed to covet their knowledge as a special ability, being reluctant to pass along information. Most of the technicians had difficulty completing admission work ups of new patients, and most had to be told time and again how to do a simple reboot after a system hangup. The computers were networked into the main hospital with ready access to all the records of its thousand of patients.

In one office, only one person, a civilian nurse, seemed to have it all together, with the result that he stayed overburdened, and overworked all of the time.

The counselors, who were most effective with their patients, admitted to be recovering. Most of the patients had difficulty relating, in a few short weeks, to someone not recovering. This thought prevailed among some of the patients: Those counselors having related degrees, but lacking actual personal experience with an addiction of their own, were seen, and feared, as experimenters rather than therapists: A new supply of guinea pigs became available on a weekly basis. To the patients, this fear was very real, and prompted me to write the story *Guinea Pig* appearing in the front of this book.

The general rule followed for admission insisted that patients had to already have been detoxified or "clean," prior to beginning their personal therapy. But sometimes this would be overlooked, and patients would be admitted while still under the influence of their drug of choice. Sometimes patients continued to use, and tested positive during their stay. On many occasions, those using drugs or drinking while in attendance, would be allowed to remain under the general excuse that "Perhaps the patient will learn something based upon his or her experience." Most of the rule-following patients I talked to agreed that this reflected badly on their own morale.

From a layman's standpoint, some of the therapy appeared to be disturbing. During one relaxation session, a patient had been regressed, that is, taken back to early childhood. She had been sexually abused by her father. The counselor had apparently not been sufficiently trained in this type of recovery technique, and could not bring the patient back to present reality quickly. The patient ran from the center, and fantasized for several hours.

The other patients seemed uncertain as to what this type of therapy tried to discover with a patient in substance abuse recovery lasting only several weeks. Some of the other patients stayed visibly affected, and understandably frightened, by the results of this procedure for some time after the session. This incident dominated their private discussion topics for several days. They feared one of them might be next. Could the counselor have been practicing for another position?

Another peculiar approach to therapy, centered around patients removing their clothing in front of the group participants, in a demonstration of being able to go to any length for their recovery. Asked first to what extent a patient would go, the decision had to be made between either jumping from a high place or removing clothing. Obviously, the first is unthinkable so the second choice is usually accepted. Oddly enough, patients who had removed their clothing during these sessions, admitted during their AA meetings to doing this, and further stated that their feelings of confidence had been elevated by the act.

One other unusual technique stands out, not only in my mind, but supported by other patients as well.

Some counselors employed a scare tactic, that is, they threatened to have the patient summarily discharged if improvement in his or her recovery program wasn't forthcoming.

Recall earlier that I said treatment has been limited to an average of three weeks, and that sometimes, patients would be allowed to remain after using, drinking while in treatment, or initially admitted without being fully detoxified.

A clear head is paramount in any recovery situation, and a threat of outright fear can only serve to reinforce a patient's uncertainty as to what recovery is all about. In three weeks, most patients are lucky if they detoxify substantially, and end up having some small idea of who they are, and what they might become.

Lack of Step One progress is usually the cause for issuing the scare tactic. Step One is the critical step—with the belief that all the other steps mean little or nothing, if Step One isn't understood.

Simply admitting isn't enough–it goes much further. The realization of what Step One is all about must be experienced, indeed it must be lived to be understood.

Some recovering people believe Step One is the only criterion necessary for a good recovery program, that all the following steps are simply nothing more than another addiction replacing the original. They feel that the end result of good recovery therapy should produce a person free from *all* addictions.

Some recovering people I know admit to not yet being satisfied with their own Step One progress, and yet, they have years of sober recovery to their credit.

Nobody passes or graduates from a recovery program, and there is no cure from alcoholism. I find it hard to believe that three weeks of threats aid anybody's recovery, regardless of the level of addiction possessed when coming into a program.

Scare tactics, I feel, simply cause the patient to fake his or her progress–leaving little foundation to work from once leaving the center. Put on paper, records show that the patient demonstrated significant progress in understanding, and working Step One, so the record looks good. If this is typical of other centers, how does anyone get the proper motivation to begin, and stay with a good recovery program? Remember, I said the word **want** is all important.

Patients need help and encouragement to aid in their progress, not fear-driven "whipping" to force out results.

Few, if any, counselors seemed to have an interest in patients after their release, leaving it to the system to take follow-up action. During my last treatment, I signed a paper stating that I would be happy to participate in ongoing monitoring of my recovery progress on a semiannual basis for a period of five years. I'm successfully sober for over nine years, and have received only one query. This alleged lack of interest lead me to believe that nobody cared, but I don't believe it's had much effect on my overall recovery program.

Others do not have much influence on what I do, only I can change myself.

The requirement for all patients to attend local AA and NA meetings on a regular basis, usually at night, five days a week seemed of significant importance to me. However, even this suffered from local policy. Originally, a large bus with a driver had been provided. The NAs would be dropped off at their respective meeting, and then the AAs would be dropped off. Pickup occurred in the reverse order an hour and a half later.

With the reduction of funding, the big bus and the driver were replaced with two smaller vans with drivers. This degraded further, with the assigned military drivers being replaced by patients who had a driver's license. The vans always seemed to need gas, and the credit cards always seemed to be missing. Finally, somebody decided that the tech or nurse on duty would accompany the patients each night to their respective meetings. Another, bigger, problem surfaced–there being only one duty person and two vans. One group always managed to get off with no supervision.

In addition, the duty person would normally not be a recovering person, and the presence of a "nonalcoholic" at some AA meetings detracted from the regular fellowship attendees discussing their concerns as much as they ordinarily might have done. This procedure also put a hardship on the duty person, since this clean individual had to be involuntarily exposed to the unfamiliar proceedings of AA or NA meetings.

Patients would be required to obtain the name of a temporary sponsor while at these meetings, and would then be allowed to leave during weekends in the company of the sponsor if they properly checked out. Checkout consisted of a clipboard hanging on a nail outside the nurse's station. On many occasions, patients checked out without being accompanied by their temporary sponsor, or fake names would be used.

The requirement for obtaining a temporary sponsor, I felt, proved to be an excellent one when properly employed, since it allowed for a better recovery approach to be practiced. Being in a treatment or recovery center for such a limited time at best allows only for a period of discovery, certainly not one of recovery. The benefit of a sponsor having a long number of twenty-four sober, and recovering hours is extremely encouraging to new patients.

We had a saying: *Anyone can sober up, it only takes twenty-four hours, recovery will take the rest of our lives.* If I had not had the opportunity to experience firsthand, addiction, then sobriety, and finally discovery showing the way to recovery, I would not have had the opportunity to appreciate all the remarkably good things in life, and the ability to seek and appreciate all of them. In this respect, I am eternally grateful to my sponsor and friend.

Patients cheated the system, and so did some of the staff. Generally, overall supervision was conspicuous by its absence—remember, I spent twenty-four years in the Marines.

In a separate recovery center, the bars around the doors and windows afforded some control of patient traffic, but the main door was seldom locked, except after taps. In hospitals, there are few locks on main doors, the patient's individual rooms, and they can be opened from the inside without a key anyway. Normal policy is to only lock these doors whenever the patients are away from the ward attending meetings. This is for protection of their personal property, rather than for traffic control. Up to four patients may share one room, and come and go as they please.

In one of my attempts at recovery, I definitely received the feeling that one of the critical inputs for married addicts had been to encourage divorce. It just so happened that the two big advocates of this technique had been recently divorced, and both had remarried. Both professed to be recovering. It is also interesting to note that in all my attendance at various AA fellowships around town, I had only seen one counselor, who admitted to be recovering, out of all those I had been associated with, at a meeting.

One of the things that group participation attempts to get across is a noticeable improvement of some single person by the other group members. This serves as an impetus similar to, "If he/

she can do it, so can I." But this reflection also extends beyond the favorable–a reverse reflection can have a similar, if not stronger impetus for wanting to recover. Seeing no recovery, or constant relapse over and over, can be equally effective. Here it comes out as, "Boy, I really don't want to go through all the things that person seems to be going through." Group participation is a big factor in aiding recovering people.

Patients, particularly during the first several weeks of their recovery, need empathetic, or at least sympathetic relationships to renew their faith with the world. The world is, after all, made up of people, and this reinforcement can play a critical role in whether or not a patient develops a positive attitude to take along after leaving the treatment center. Getting everyone together to play games, or have a barbeque, is not socializing in the way that I mean it. A family atmosphere existed in the "back porch" discussions I was privileged to attend during my stay at my last recovery attempt. This type of atmosphere certainly played a significant role in my own recovery program. It consisted entirely of patients. It was here, on the back porch, in this family atmosphere, that I found the motivation for wanting my recovery.

Exercise is good, also participation in organized sports, but there is no substitute for good old family atmosphere. Here patients can let it all hang out, and ask and receive answers for highly personal questions. I felt that this family atmosphere we made for ourselves even went beyond the expressed openness usually present at AA meetings. For recovering patients, people at AA meetings are new friends, here, on the back porch, they are *old* and *trusted* friends, a significant difference. To this day, even though I haven't seen many of them lately, I have an eternal gratitude to my old back porch friends.

8

Patients perspective

It was 2145 hours, and the group had just returned from their regularly scheduled AA meeting. One by one each patient drifted onto the second floor porch adjoining the "old folks" side of the house. Each patient carried a hardbound file with a blue or red cover. Seven patients came this evening for the back porch discussion. Bill S arrived last.

"Anybody have any trouble getting your records?" he asked of the group as a whole.

"Naw," said Willie, "the tech on duty is in the patient's lounge watchin' TV." At 65, and on his seventh attempt at recovery, he was the oldest of the patients in the current cycles attending treatment. In addition to his alcohol treatment, he needed insulin shots for diabetes twice a day. He had created quite a stir when the other patients in the ward saw him sticking himself: They had seen a recovering addict casually loading a syringe and shooting himself up.

"Let's all get closer together in a group and we'll begin," Bill said.

"Did you know," Hondo said, "that three people died in this hospital over the past week?" An Air Force captain, Hondo worked in some sort of ground control approach capacity in another state.

"How do you know that?" Marty, the youngest at nineteen, asked.

A spec four, and retired general's only daughter, her mother now took care of Marty's two little girls. As one of her bigger problems, Marty tried to cope with not knowing who the fathers were.

"When that same tech who's in the TV lounge sits at the nurse's station," Hondo said, "he plays games on the computer that's in there. I went in earlier, tried to find a game, and arbitrarily hit some keys. All of a sudden I looked at hospital records. All sorts of neat information is in there."

"Did you see what our records said?" Marty asked.

"No," said Hondo, "I didn't know how to move around in the program and besides, I had to exit quickly, I heard the duty nurse coming."

"Well, maybe it's better if you stay out of there completely," Bill said, "we all have enough of our own problems without getting caught in somebody's confidential files."

"You think those files are classified?" Willie asked.

"I would hope so," said Bill, "I certainly wouldn't want just anybody looking at my record whenever he wanted to."

"They sure seem to handle things funny around here," Willie said.

"Why did we bring our records here tonight?" Claude asked. Claude was dual-addicted, would leave on the next flight out, and go back to his own unit in Alabama.

"We want to make a comparison of something Willie and I were talking over for some time now," Bill said.

After about a half hour of looking at the records, and making comparisons, everyone agreed that the record for each of them sounded more or less the same.

"Why do you suppose that is?" Marty asked.

"We have a theory," Willie said. "First of all, notice that all the information is on a standard form used by the center. The only real differences besides our names, are the numbers and results of all the tests they run on us while we're in here. Our theory is that since we all have the same disease, the disease of addiction, all the treatment would be the same. It looks like it's as if we're all the same person."

"But if it's a standard form," Hondo said, "how come the book is almost two inches thick?"

"Somebody's trying to cover their ass," Marty said. "You know the military, and all its paperwork. The more confusing they can make it, the less chance of getting caught if they make a mistake."

"You really are cynical," Claude said.

Marty's eyes lit up, and she said, "Yep, that's one of the interventions they have me working on right now."

Bill said, "What did you all think about the meeting we went to tonight?"

A brief break in the conversation ensued while everyone looked at everyone else, and finally, a few admitted that they had thought it had been a good meeting.

"That's just the point," Bill said. "It *was* a good meeting. Did you hear all that deep stuff those two at the end of the big table talked about? Yet both of them have different ideas about their respective recoveries."

"That's just what point?" Hondo asked.

Bill started explaining.

"Willie and I have been discussing this for a while. We're told over and over to keep things simple aren't we?" Without waiting for an answer from anyone he continued. "Imagine if, when we arrived at that meeting tonight, somebody had just handed us a small card with the words *DON'T DRINK* printed on it, and then asked us to return again next week. Wouldn't you all have felt cheated? But, 'don't drink' is exactly the message we are supposed to get from all the meetings and counseling sessions we have."

Willie picked it up from here. "All our lives we have been complicating things," he said," it's the only thing we know how to do well. Did you know there are 916 letters in the Twelve Steps? I counted 'em. If you stirred all those letters up, and just selected nine of them, you could spell the words, 'don't drink.' To reduce the Twelve Step Program to two simple words would take away the effectiveness of the entire program."

"For me to understand what I need in this recovery program," Bill said, "I think it's necessary that I study, and take some of this information slowly. Perhaps later, when, and if I'm still sober many years from now, I'll be able to simplify things down to a few short words. Here, I feel that I'm treated no different than anybody else, but at meetings I find that I'm unique. I need to start working on myself as an individual. I must stay sober my way, not the center's way."

"Wow," Geoffrey said, "I didn't think of looking at it that way." So far he hadn't said much, being new, and nobody knew anything about him.

"I look forward to these meetings we have on this porch," Bill Said. "If it wasn't for the way we all discuss, and help interpret some of the things that we hear each day, I feel certain that I would miss a whole hell of a lot of good information."

"So do I," Marty agreed, "I was totally lost when I first came here, and you guys helped me a lot, 'specially with my cards."

"Speaking of cards," Geoffrey said, "I have a bunch to fill out, and I haven't the vaguest idea where to start. Also, what's a Time Line, and as long as I'm asking for help, what do I put on this sheet with the thermometer on it?"

"Don't sweat that stuff," Hondo said, "I'll help you with it all, I'm a master at Time Lines. I'll even give you my colored pencils."

"Thanks," Geoffrey said.

"Getting back to what you were talking about, Bill," Hondo said. "Maybe I've been looking at this recovery of mine all wrong."

"Me too," Claude said, "I'm glad we had this meeting here on the porch right before I leave. I'll certainly remember to start looking at things differently from now on."

Marty didn't say anything, but the others could see her thinking hard. Finally she took her own stack of cards, and spread them out on the table.

"My counselor has me going in circles with these cards," she said. "Look at some of her comments."

Words had been written in red over Marty's pencil notations. *Get real, grow up, do you really believe this?,* and *you're absolutely lost here,* were some that they all could see.

"I don't know what to do," Marty said. "She tells me I'm wrong, but won't tell me what to do about it. Yesterday, I came up here, and cried after class, I felt so lonely."

Again, thoughts of Patient Y came to Bill's mind, and he silently thanked her.

"Just now, what you just did is a good thing," he said. "You're confused, and have asked for help. I think that's part of what our recovery is all about–not being afraid to ask for help."

He reached for the cards, and looked around the little group.

"Let's all take a crack at some of these, and see what we can come up with," he said.

For about an hour the group attacked the information on the cards. Then they discussed each point with Marty. Some of the other patients made notes of their own as the critique went along. Finally, they all agreed on a short break.

Once they had all gathered around again, Bill said, "Did any of you ever stop and think how much time your counselors, and all the hired help around here, spend on you individually? We're always in a group of more than eight in size, and some days nobody makes any requirement of me to talk or discuss anything at all. I do get a chance to listen a lot. I feel that I learn more from these porch discussions than from anywhere else, even the AA meetings."

"I haven't seen that one shrink but once since I've been here," Hondo said, "and then all he did was ask me if I felt depressed? I said 'Hell yes, that's why I'm here.' I don't feel like I'm getting my money's worth, at least from him, and he probably makes a hundred grand a year. How much do you suppose it costs to keep us here for six weeks anyway?"

Willie–"The VA pays $1,000 a day for us retired folks."

Marty–"I'm glad daddy doesn't have to pay for my treatment out of his own pocket, he probably wouldn't do it after all the trouble I've caused."

Willie–"My expenses are approaching the national debt."

"We're all searching for something," Bill said, "something we've never had–feelings of self-worth, and of being wanted. The only family atmosphere I get around here is from these porch gatherings. I think I learn more about myself up here than I do even from all the AA meetings."

"My father always treated me like another soldier," Marty said, "I'm thankful that I was sent here for one thing anyway. I'm thankful that you guys are giving me the family that I never had. Maybe that's the big reason I was sent here."

"We all love you," Bill said.

"That's another thing we get from up here," Willy said. "I haven't heard so many 'I love you's in a long time. Come to think of it, I haven't heard those words around my house in a long time either."

"I feel a definite change in my overall attitude since I've been here," Hondo said. "I feel closer to all of you at this table than to all the people I work with put together, and I've been with some of them for years."

"I've been hugged ten times today already," Geoffrey said, "and I don't even know ten peoples' names."

Silence existed among the little group for a long while.

"Well," Bill finally said, "it's getting late, let's all wander out of here and get our records back one or two at a time. We'll meet again tomorrow night."

"If the tech is still in the TV room," Hondo said," I'm going to try my luck at that computer again."

"I need another insulin," Willie said, "then it's the sack for me."

Before retiring, Bill sat on the back porch, and thought for a long while. He realized that he felt better than he had in a long time. This feeling went beyond the lift that he received from a good workout. He equated the feeling as being similar to the high he used to feel each time he began a drinking bout.

He hadn't been drinking for a long while, and realized that the high had come from the exhilaration he had received from helping Marty with her cards. He thought that he also received this elation whenever he attended an AA meeting. In fact, he recalled always feeling better when he left a meeting, even though he had felt good before going. These uplifting feelings started becoming something he wanted to continue. He had an inkling that for the first time in his life, he might be on the right track. He could get high without alcohol.

9

Reality

Bill S once again sat on the porch in deep thought. For the past week he had been involved in a significant modification with his recovery program: A seed of change had been planted, only he didn't completely realize it yet. He had been discussing his progress with his sponsor.

"When you go to these compulsory meetings," his sponsor had asked him, "do you speak?"

"Of course, I feel obligated to say something at each and every meeting that I attend," Bill had answered.

"Maybe that's it," his sponsor had said, "I had something of a similar problem. You spend half your time at the meeting thinking up what you want to say. After you say it, you spend the other half of the time thinking how you could have said it better. The net result is that you're not hearing the meeting."

Bill hadn't answered, but he thought about what his sponsor had said.

"Do me a favor," his sponsor had said, "make a pact with me. For the next week, whenever you're at a meeting, don't say anything, just listen."

Bill had said yes, and mentioned to his counselors and fellow patients at his next group session, that he wanted to do this. Oddly enough, they all honored the pact–he hadn't been called upon to say anything for an entire week, even during his counseling sessions. He couldn't define it, being barely aware of it at this time, but a profound change began to grow within.

Hondo arrived, and from the way his eyebrows were set and his eyes looked, Bill guessed that something bothered him.

"You look puzzled," Bill said.

"These people are going to keep me here another week," Hondo replied. "My counselor says I'm not doing Step One correctly. How the hell does he know what's right, he's not recovering?"

"Sit down," Bill said. "And take the load off. It's obvious you're upset, and right now you don't need that. I've been doing some thinking along these lines myself for the past week. How old are you?"

"Thirty-seven," Hondo answered.

"And how long have you been involved with alcohol?" Bill asked.

"Nineteen years," was the reply.

"So," Bill said, "half your life has been controlled by alcohol. Have you taken a good look at yourself lately?"

"Every morning," Hondo said smiling, "when I shave for Uncle Sam."

"Well," Bill said, "you might not see any change, but I certainly notice a big difference from the first day when you walked in here. Why do you suppose that is?"

"I don't know," Hondo said, "I've been eating better, and I hit the gym more now than I ever did."

"There it is," Bill said, "you didn't answer the question." For a brief moment, an image of the fat civilian from Okinawa appeared in Bill's mind. "I think the main reason that you look better is that you haven't had any alcohol in over a month."

"I never thought about that," Hondo said.

"Precisely my point, you're not thinking correctly," said Bill. "After nineteen years of drinking, when do you think this magic cure you're looking for will be discovered, on the day you walk out of this recovery center?"

"I guess I never thought about that either," Hondo said.

"But you certainly have been thinking about a lot of things while you've been in here, right?" Bill said.

"You bet," Hondo said, "about how to do Step One correctly for this guy so he'll let me leave for one thing."

"Why don't you just fake it like so many other patients are doing?" Bill asked. "Just tell them what they want to hear, and you'll be out."

"But that would be cheating the system," Hondo said.

"A good point, take some credit for yourself." Bill said. "Earlier, I didn't think the system cared, one way or the other, now I'm not so sure. I do think that if we fail after leaving here, they will blame us, and if we don't fail they'll take the credit. We, on the other hand, will blame them if we fail, and we'll take the credit, ourselves, if we don't. But who will know besides us, if our program is effective or not, unless we're like that guy in group three who's back in again after seven months."

"All the fellows I work with will know," Hondo said.

"Want to bet?" Bill said. "How many people do you work with?"

"Nine," Hondo answered.

"So," Bill said, "nine people will have nine different expectations of how you should show your recovery. Which one will you choose?"

"I'm getting your point," Hondo said. "I have to recover my way if it is to do me any good."

"And which way will you be working Step One?" Bill asked.

"Ha!" Hondo said, "my way exactly, or it won't mean anything will it?"

"I think that's a basic point we're not taught here," Bill said. "I feel that the best thing I can do for myself is not drink any more alcohol. If I concentrate on not drinking, I will be working Step One in my own way even if I don't understand the step, and if anybody sees me they will notice the difference. That's a big change that I think I've just started learning about myself this past week. Maybe that's the point of all this treatment."

"So, I think I'll concentrate on that approach," Hondo said, "another week isn't so long."

"Your desk won't even show any more thickness of dust than it already has on it," Bill said. "What do you feel is going to be our biggest challenge when we leave here?"

"Working with all the steps in our programs," Hondo said.

"During my first attempt at recovery," Bill said, "I didn't know much about the Twelve-Step Program. But I did notice that nobody out there among the 'normies' really seemed to care one way or the other if I worked at any kind of program. I found out then, that the word *alcoholic* carries an underlying tone of something bad, and a negative ring or stigma is automatically attached to it. It usually keeps people like us from seeking help in the first place. Mention a Twelve Step Program to a 'normie,' and he'd look at me funny, and get quickly away."

"Something like my counselors," Hondo said, "they can't understand how bad craving and withdrawal can make us feel, and they certainly can't feel how much we don't want to go back out there."

"I think my biggest problem, once I leave here," Bill said, "will happen right at the time I walk away from this treatment center. If I don't crash immediately, I figure I'll have a chance. I'll probably drive my sponsor nuts right in the beginning. It is a real world, and so far my life has been one big fantasy. I expect I'll want, and need a lot of help."

The seed continued to grow as the new outlook on his new life began taking shape within Bill S.

"Speaking of your Step One progress," Bill said, "my sponsor asked me once what I felt was the most important word in the step."

"That's easy," Hondo said, "There are two, *powerless* and *unmanageable*."

"He had a little different interpretation," Bill said. "My sponsor said that the word *lives* is in there, and nothing could be any more important to recovering people than their own lives. I've been doing a lot of thinking on that point. It's all part of changing how I want to look at things now"

The seed kept growing.

"I still remember," Bill said, "sitting on a bar stool next to another person, and releasing all of my hostilities, frustrations, and inhibitions over a glass of beer. I used to solve all the world's problems that way. The thing was, that the next day, all the problems would still be there. In reality, nothing had been solved, but I thought I felt better. Now I'm beginning my recovery program. I've substituted words like 'sharing' and 'relating' for 'wailing' and 'crying,' and the surroundings are different, but nothing significant seems to have changed. The one big difference is that the glass in empty! Right now I seem to have more difficulty than I did before, and the damn stuff isn't even there."

"Don't I know it," Hondo agreed.

"Why can't I draw on all the power and determination I used to have before whenever I wanted a drink? After all, I used to go to any length to get it. Now that same power and determination seem to be no longer available, even though there is probably nothing wrong with my physical and mental makeup, other than a significant amount of denial remaining. I feel that I must draw on my behavioral abilities to ask for help from others. By doing, thinking, and feeling new thoughts, I can get on with this process of healing. AA meetings will help, but I still am reminded that the glass is empty. Such is the power of alcohol."

From one of his Marine Corps training definitions, Bill liked to equate the protection he got from alcohol to the protection that concealment provides versus cover. Cover keeps one from being shot, concealment simply keeps one from being seen, and not likely to be shot at. There is a difference. In the case of the concealment protection of alcohol, Bill now felt that he could be shot at and hit, if he hadn't been already.

He wasn't drinking now, and he felt that the likelihood of drinking would be nil as long as he stayed here within the confines of the recovery center. But, the world is still real, and he would leave some day, more likely sooner than later. His fear of change was real.

He continued as if Hondo wasn't there.

"I feel," Bill said, "that the most important thing I can do right now, is to make an honest effort to stay away from trying to manipulate and control my own recovery, and to allow it to lay before me whatever is intended to happen. Then I must endeavor to deal with the choices offered.

"I have the feeling that most of the staff here is conscientious, and that they believe in what they're doing. I think the counselors feel the approach is right. Some have been here for years, maybe we're just not hearing what they're saying in the right way. A few bad ones always crop up—something we'll have to deal with in real life from now on."

"When I hear you say things this way," Hondo said, "I realize just how big this recovery business is going to be. I think, so far, that I've been laughing at it in an attempt to ignore it."

"This is our period of discovery," Bill said, "just that. We're not here any longer for it to go any farther. Each of us must make our own discovery about ourselves, and at our own pace, if it is to have any lasting effect on our recovery. All our lives we have been rejecting whatever people threw at us. It's no different now, and we have to allow ourselves to change."

These discussions on the porch helped. Here, away from any supervision, people are more likely to unload on what and how they really felt. A little bit of reality existed here on this porch. At other places the environment always seemed to him to be controlled to some extent. Perhaps it existed now in the only way he could look at it, and would change along with other changes he would find necessary to be made in his new life.

Addictive diseases behave in strange ways, and professional people are only beginning to understand some of the effects. Psychologically, the alcoholic's mind keeps being told that he or she doesn't have a disease—that it is the others, the non-drinkers, or the controlled drinkers that are at fault. Two very different classes of people are affected: The direct victim of the disease, the alcoholic, as in Bill's case, and the indirect victims, all the other members of society. To make any progress, these other people must be educated as well.

Bill S realized he had been wrong in many of his initial impressions of this treatment center–his stinking thinking had still been in charge. It began to dawn on him that he couldn't begin his recovery program alone, and the counselors' external help now seemed to be a key input into his recovery program. At least it alerted him to the things that are provided to help him on his way. All he, or any of them, need do, is let it happen. Recovery is easier if someone shows the way. Getting to the end is up to the individual, but the journey is where all the important progress will happen.

10

Acceptance

We, as human beings, live in a real world. It exists outside of us, and we can only experience this real world through sensory perceptions. From what we see, hear, smell, taste, and feel, we construct an impression of all the real stuff of the world. We do this on such a deep and instinctive level, modified by experience and memory, that we say we know, or can understand the real world.

My brain weighs three and one-half pounds, yet I have what I feel to be a rather complete conception of what the cosmological universe is. But my impression is only consciously formed, so, in a sense, all my knowledge of everything is abstract. Does that mean that the universe only weighs three and one-half pounds? Of course not.

Since adopting a successful recovery program, I've had to develop a new approach, a new way to look at things. I must make an effort to discover all the immediate realities that become dear to my ultimate understandings—a different way of looking at things.

So I say I am alcoholic. *I am alcoholic.* Let me say it again, *I am alcoholic.* You know, I had trouble with that in the beginning, admitting being alcoholic. In fact, for the first several meetings I attended, I wouldn't even say that dreaded nine-letter word. But as some of the poisons gradually left my brain and body, I began to admit that OK, I may be alcoholic, *But it isn't my fault.*

Then, as still more of the poisons left, I would admit not only to being alcoholic, and that it might be my fault, but *I didn't have any DWIs.* For a long time I admitted, but did not accept; I still maintained some sort of control over my condition by attempting to qualify or justify it. Now I am comfortable wherever I may be, to admit freely and proudly, that *I am alcoholic.* If I hadn't broken my anonymity, how would anyone get to read this book?

But what does that really mean? If I am alcoholic now, after many a twenty-four-hour period of sobriety, what had I been before, when I drank constantly? After all, I spent almost fifty-two years of my life, more than half a century, either going to a drunk, being drunk, or coming away from a drunk. We have non-alcoholic beer and wine, is there such a thing as being a non-alcoholic alcoholic? I did the only thing my science-oriented brain could think of at the time, I went to the dictionary.

Alcohol is defined chemically as C_2H_5OH and it never changes. In the dictionary I used, the small three-letter suffix, *ism*, had many definitions, but the one I took with me said *state or condition resulting from an excess of something.* Then, at a meeting, I heard that alcoholism is a disease. So there it is, my condition is the result of a disease that is caused by too much alcohol. But what kind of a disease is it? Consider the following:

If a group of people suddenly breaks out in chicken pox, everyone will get the same symptoms, those small, itchy bumps all over. The symptoms are treated by calamine lotion, in several days the disease goes away, and a funny thing happens: The chance of catching the chicken pox again becomes remote. The people develop an immunity simply by having the disease.

If a group of people suddenly catches the flu, everyone will get the same symptoms: muscle soreness, cough, run down feeling, and again, they will treat the symptoms, and in about a week the people will get better. But having the flu once is no assurance that one can never catch it again. Indeed, some people have the flu over and over each year. A vaccine, in the form of an inoculation, can assist in reducing the probability of catching the flu.

We have two different diseases that everyone can get, giving all those afflicted the same symptoms, which are treated, and the diseases go away. One disease is usually never caught again, and the other can be immunized against.

Now, consider the disease of alcoholism. All those afflicted with this disease get the same symptoms: relaxed inhibitions, elevated feelings of pleasure, false sense of security, false courage, anxiety, craving, a progressive muscular and mental debilitation, and finally, addiction, and if untreated, death. Most of us recovering folks can relate firsthand to the feelings of withdrawal.

Treating the symptoms is of no help. Sure, a shot, or "hair of the dog" is temporary, but is by no means an inoculation against catching the disease again. There is no immunity to be had from initially catching the Disease of Alcoholism. Also, since the disease is progressive, we can only get worse, never better. Therefore, a different approach is necessary. We must consider treating the disease itself, not the symptoms. How do we do this? How do we treat the *ism*, or the addiction? This is where another way of looking at things comes in.

In treatment, we were encouraged to follow the same Twelve-Step Program used by Alcoholics Anonymous. It offers a few simple guidelines consisting of twelve principles called steps. Since we are human, we usually begin with Step One.

Step One says, "We admitted we were powerless over alcohol, that our lives had become unmanageable." For some recovering alcoholics, Step One is the only relevant step.

Step One is where I had to give up my control. There are thirteen words in Step One and the word *control* is not one of them. Where does it say in Step One that I should give up control over anything? In fact, why should I give up my control at all? I didn't do too badly during my life of drinking, throughout my Marine Corps career, and later in civilian life. I made lots of money, did some impressive things, raised four children, and retired at the age of fifty-nine to a planned retirement paradise in a rather scenic locale that included a thirteen-mile view of a river. But I missed something, my control had brought me into three recovery centers.

Whenever I look at Step One, I see the word *control* in between the lines. I also see other words that are there but not written. Words like *surrender, acceptance, honesty,* and *believe.* For me, Step One is the stepping off place that allowed me to reevaluate my life and change its direction. The changes come in accordance with my newfound wisdom. It is a wisdom that allows me to understand, and to say good things about myself. I want to do this. I am unique, there is nobody else on Earth exactly like I am. Today, a different kind of control plays a big part in my new way of looking at things.

During treatment I remember being subjected to an experiment. As we sat in our familiar circle, each in turn had been asked to say nice things about ourselves. Then, each in turn had been asked to say awful or unpleasant things. The second list turned out to be much longer, and much easier to say.

The next two steps in the recommended series involve adopting, or living through, a psychic or spiritual change. Of course I also had difficulty with these steps. For most of my life I never thought enough about a God, or a spiritual outlook, to even be considered an atheist. But I learned. Again, in treatment we were encouraged to seek an external source of spiritual energy.

I learned that I didn't have to accept anyone else's ideas. I learned that I could adopt my own concept. In an approach similar to Patient Y's want ad, I went about my search for what most of us called a Higher Power, in a rather unorthodox fashion however.

To assist in driving the idea into my mind that there is an external source of energy out there, I took my Higher Power, and put it in a box. Then I carried the box with me everywhere I went. It always would be available as long as I had the box, and by being in the box, it certainly supported the concept of something external. I proudly showed my box at meetings.

One day I wrote the words *surrender, acceptance, honesty,* and *believe* on the bottom of the box. And I went through a stage where I was sure that I was my own Higher Power. After all, I put those words in the box, and they helped me whenever I called upon them. Then I noticed something. Sometimes, when I couldn't completely solve a problem, right a wrong or salve a wound, I would turn it over to my Higher Power, and *somehow* it got done without my influence, from something outside of me. I had to modify my way of looking at things again. If there really is such a Higher Power, that Higher Power certainly didn't need my help getting in or out of my box. I continued my search. An Army Chaplain helped.

He conducted a class called Spiritual Replenishment, and I ended up assisting him for about eighteen months while I searched. One day as we sat in our usual circle awaiting his presence, he arrived late . . . deliberately. He had brought with him a small black case from which he withdrew two pieces of a musical instrument. Never saying a word, he went through slow, deliberate motions of assembling this instrument, and then, majestically, placed it on a table in front of us. He asked if it didn't look beautiful? We all agreed that, in fact, the clarinet did look beautiful.

He asked what it did, and we all agreed that it made beautiful music. To the first response he replied, "Right," but to the second he said, "Wrong. By itself it just sits there. It needs to be coupled to an external source of energy before it can make beautiful music." Thereupon he picked up the instrument, and proceeded to play it. We all sang along to some of the songs as he played.

That display caught my attention. I needed to find a Higher Power that the clarinet symbolically represented, and off I went on my quest, looking for something that I could couple to and begin making beautiful music. I did this for about a year, looking for a symbolic clarinet, until one day I realized that I could stop looking–I am the clarinet! External energy coupling to me is the way it works, and it can come from almost anywhere: The power in the group, an individual, a simple thought, and even the Higher Power that I had inappropriately relegated to my small box years ago.

I had found yet another way of looking at things. The key to shifting my spiritual focus required me to have an open mind, and to allow myself to experience something different, much like conducting an experiment with my spiritual life. An important word in my spiritual readjustment was the word *surrender*. In this case, it doesn't mean going belly up. I had to surrender myself to the highest aspect of my ability to rediscover my new world of values and beliefs. As I change my spiritual focus, I will necessarily develop a different lifestyle because what is important to me has changed. Spirituality provides a new basis for all my decisions and relationships, but at the same time, I'm not a devoutly religious person. I follow no single dogma. It makes no difference what title I give to my new spiritual assistance program: Belief in a religious God, a God of a new understanding, an external Higher Power that comes from groups of other recovering persons, or just a simple recognition that this external source of energy is something or someone other than me. I have faith in something that I don't fully understand, and that's all right.

My Higher Power operates on a random reinforcement basis. Its standards are not mine, and they come at no specific time. I talk to my Higher Power, and I talk to others about my Higher Power. We have no trouble understanding, yet I can't loan it to anyone, or use my credit card to purchase one.

When I buy a new suit, and stand in front of the tailor's three mirrors to check its overall fit, I see an image of myself. I do not see myself as I actually am. By looking in the mirror I see a fake version of me. The same is true for my understanding of my Higher Power. If I look at only the image, I see only a fake version.

I need to somehow remove my eyes from myself, place them away from my body, and view myself as I actually am. Only in that manner will I obtain a true version of what I see. Since I can't remove my eyes, I must try and look at myself from the inside out. It's not as easy, but I find that with more and more practice, I can go beyond the image, and begin looking at me as I actually am. I need not be satisfied trying to comprehend anything fake. So I keep looking.

Sometimes I feel we are all victims of what I call the Chipmunk Syndrome. We've all had occasion to see a little chipmunk dart in front of our vehicle as we drove along a road, usually at night, and outside of the city. But did you ever consider what is going through the chipmunk's mind from the chipmunk's point of view? Perhaps it would be something like this:

For a long while, he had sat poised by the edge of the road. Traffic had been flowing steadily for the entire time. He had spent the time preparing himself for the immediate task to come. He wanted very much to cross the road and to get to the other side. This side was all right, but he just knew that it would be better on the other side. He was sure if it. If anything, the ground would no doubt be drier than on this side. He shivered. He stuck his head up higher, looking around as far as he could see. There wasn't much to the traffic pattern that could be seen, it simply didn't stop. He would have to dart quickly across during one of the gaps. Several times before he had almost tried, but just at the right moment he canceled the desire to be rewarded by the immediate whoosh of a passing vehicle. But he had to go sometime. He looked around again, . . . nothing. He bolted.

As fast as he could, he darted out from the protection of the short grass on this side of the road, and ran over the hard, black surface. The rough texture hurt his feet. He ran, faster and faster. He crossed the halfway point without any mishap, and continued to run. He was going to make it, everything would be all right. Things would definitely be better on the other side.

Now he was almost across. He thought how nice it would be on the other side. But would it? He had no way of knowing this. Now he wasn't so sure. He wasn't certain of anything. He knew it was all right on the side he had just left, but this would be a completely new place. He continued to run. What would be the danger he might have to face? Second thoughts began entering his mind. He stopped, stood straight up on his hind legs, and looked around. Vehicles sped in both directions around him.

He became frightened. Maybe he had been better off, after all, on the original side. More vehicles sped past. He really was scared now, not only from the traffic, but also from the unknown on the new side. He had been familiar with the area on the original side of the road. There he found comfort in the things he knew. Perhaps this had been a bad choice after all, for him to make the dash for the new side.

These things went through his mind almost as fast as the traffic sped around him. He had been much better off on the original side. He was sure of it.

He panicked.

He would go back.

On all fours again, he began running back to the original side of the road. He had changed his mind, and now he ran as fast as he could, to get back to his old way of life.

There is the constant fear of the unknown. If our little chipmunk gets clobbered on the return trip, as is likely, he will have lost what he had on the original side as well as what he might have had on the new side. Risks are an important input to my recovery, and offer the freedom that I need to progress and grow in my newfound, and sober life. I must cross over to the new side. But I need not understand everything for things to work out.

Among my fellow recovering alcoholics there is a universal understanding that benefit comes, usually without asking, and that to just let it happen seems to be the easiest and most effective way. My recovery program proceeds at a pace that I've become accustomed to, and I currently see no reason to modify anything at the moment. I realize however, that just as my previous ideas about my Higher Power concept necessarily had to change, so shall they change again as I continue to grow and learn.

With this newfound wisdom, I can honestly say that I like myself, something I couldn't do before. I enjoy being me, I am a nice person. I am more optimistic and more extroverted. I am more selective to the type of friends I have, I have a greater sense of spirituality, and above all, I am no longer lonely. Now, free and liberated, I believe I've found my way.

Abstaining from alcohol is the only way for me to treat my disease.

I met a friend the other day who left treatment just as I came on board. I hadn't seen him in several years, and he looked great. I could tell immediately that he still maintained his sobriety, and his advertisement of healing in action gave me a tremendous lift. We spoke for a while, and he divulged that, at the age of 77, he was fighting prostate cancer.

"You know," he said, "there have been times over the past year when I have felt depressed with all this therapy for cancer, but never once have I had the urge to drink. You want to know why?"

"Why?" I asked.

"Because I feel good," he said. "I am sick and tired of being sick and tired, and I know that I won't feel as good if I go back to drinking."

That is the case with me today. I feel good, and I want that feeling to continue. In my search for my own recovery program, I did not find any magic words or phrases. I do what I have to do on a daily basis, and I accept any role that life might wish to impart. I make a realistic approach to reclaim all the wonderful aspects of my personal life that have been destroyed over the years by the effects of alcohol. I must live each and every day to its fullest in order to do this.

Still, these things don't come easy. I accept what, and who I am, and I must maintain a conscious effort all the time not to take in any alcohol. Not the inadvertent trace of alcohol in mouthwash, or in some food sauces, but alcohol deliberately ingested with the intent of actually enjoying its so-called benefits and attributes. I can sit and look at a bottle of alcohol all day, and it won't hurt me. I can watch others drink alcohol, and it won't hurt me. But as soon as I allow it to come inside, it starts doing a number on me. I still have the disease of alcoholism whether I drink or not.

I did not develop a positive, successful recovery program within three weeks as an in-patient. On the contrary, I was only lucky enough to discover that I wanted my recovery more than I wanted alcohol. I still am developing my recovery program. I must *WANT* to recover more than I want alcohol. The bottom line is that wishes and promises aren't enough. The pressing needs are there, but I must continue to *want,* above anything else, to stay away from my drug of choice, alcohol. How long will my newfound recovery and sobriety last? I have no idea, but I'm not afraid anymore.

As a revelatory participant of recovery, I just want to continue one day at a time. That is my speed limit. After nine years of following this course, today I'm not driving the bus.

EPILOGUE

Alcohol, or cocaine, isn't the only thing that drives people insane. There are other drugs, as well as: Gambling, lying, cheating, the quest for political power, you name it, it's out there. The old brain still has its wants and desires, and it has much patience. If, after reading this book, you still have doubts, and any misunderstanding about the disease of alcoholism, consider the following:

WHEN IS AN ALCOHOLIC?

We are going to try to determine when you became an alcoholic. I'll tell the story, you make the decision.

Sixty-two years ago, two gametes united, producing a zygote. By mitosis, it grew into an embryo which further developed into a fetus. This fetus developed from the DNA recombination of the parent cells. These cells made polypeptide chains from amino acids. They in turn made molecules of protein. This miracle, when it was born, became you. One of the two original gametes came from a parent who was alcoholic.

Were you an alcoholic at the time of your birth? Were you an alcoholic before you were born? Is there a gene for alcoholism, and if so, at what point during gestation does it activate? Did you become alcoholic sometime during the protein-generation stage? Or was it later?

As stated, you are 62 years old. You grew up from a baby. When you were little and your mouth hurt because of teething, your parents rubbed whisky on your gums to make the pain go away. Is this when you became an alcoholic?

In high school it was fashionable to drink in groups, at parties, or to impress, and influence others. Your tolerance was so high that you became the designated driver even though the term hadn't been invented yet. You finished college with the help of a military program called NEASEP. You got very drunk the night of graduation after being commissioned a second lieutenant. Did you become an alcoholic that night?

During several careers you did many impressive and good things, drinking heavily all the while. Some innovations created by you then are still in effect today. Your contact with the military kept you in good stead as you wined and dined some old cronies into spending their company's money on projects sold by your company. Alcohol was involved in more than one of these. Did you become an alcoholic during one of these hospitality suites?

You raised several children, and are a grandparent several times over. You got drunk the day your first child was born, and again the day his first child was born. Was either of these the time?

Suddenly, against all the debilitating things you continued to subject it to, your body began giving up the fight. You decided to quit drinking. When you made this decision, was this when you became an alcoholic? You quit a number of times, each lasting a short while, and each ending with a bigger and harder relapse. Which one of these made you an alcoholic?

Maybe you didn't become an alcoholic until the day of your divorce. *That* certainly was a traumatic experience.

Perhaps it happened the day you entered the Residential Treatment Center, or perhaps it happened while you were attending. Maybe it happened the day you left the facility to face the big, cruel world on your own. Which one do you suppose it was?

You've been sober and involved in a strong recovery program for almost nine years. Each time you speak at a meeting, you admit being alcoholic. Did you wait until you finished your fourth step before becoming alcoholic? Was it the first step? How about the eleventh?

How did it happen? Were you notified, say with a postcard, prior to the event? Did it just happen? Did you have anything to do with it, or did you just wake up one morning and it was there? You've had the benefit of healing, of evolving again, from the egg that grew so long ago. You've looked deep inside yourself, adapting all the old, misguided drives and strengths to newer, more positive directions. You know the exhilarating feeling of being reborn. You freely admit being an alcoholic, now, after nine years of sobriety; finally admit to feeling normal again.

But, what is normal? Was your life normal before when you were constantly drinking all the time? Was being normal first failing, then admitting and accepting it, and finally turning yourself around and trying to fix things? If that is the case, you are more normal now, as an admitted alcoholic free from the booze, than you ever were previously. Now you have the benefit of knowing what things you've missed, all the good things that were passed by the wayside, and are revealed to you. Now you have the ability to recognize what's right and pure and good. Now you have the ability to make sensible choices; to receive what you would have missed in the old days; to face life on life's terms, and to be confident of the solution.

If you make a choice, and say you became alcoholic during your college years, could you say that peer pressure, stress, or insecurity was the cause? Or were you just born to be an alcoholic? Is there any difference between the type of alcoholic you were then and what you are now? I submit there is a difference.

Once again, *When* is an Alcoholic?

CHL

APPENDIX A

My outlook on recovery began to change in a manner similar to what had happened to Patient Y. The turning point came with the critical realization that a desire for recovery must be present if any progress is to be made. As is the case with most recovering addicts, this realization didn't happen overnight. After about seven years of good solid sobriety, I was into my recovery to a point where I considered it to be solid enough to begin sharing with other recovering alcoholics. I wrote the following essays in the hope that I might reach others. I've included them in this book for whatever help they might be.

Excuses

What's my excuse going to be for today? The mirror provided a bleary-eyed reflection that looked back at me, pulled at my soul, but said nothing.

Each morning I would prepare an answer to protect me from anyone who might notice how bad I looked. Not getting enough sleep last night–Or that I suffered from constant allergies? I felt my secret was safe, but I also felt terrible. That was the way it used to be every morning for many years.

Today is my birthday. Not my biological, or bellybutton birthday, but the end of my seventh year of life without alcohol. It happened when I finally admitted that too much drinking had caused too much pain to the people I loved. With my new-found confidence, I no longer require any excuses to explain my condition.

Today I can say I have turned my life around by simply being my new self. My wishes and promises weren't enough. What my program needed was an honest approach to want to ask for help for myself from others. I get my encouragement from seeing my own progress. This helps me to heal and progress even more.

Today, although still silent, my reflection fairly yells a message of healing not to be denied.

Not everyone has the chance to witness miracles. I see one every time I look in a mirror. I feel good.

Thoughts

The person sitting on the curb holding a paper bag that hid a beer wasn't me. I wore a suit and tie, and drove a motor home. My beer was in the fridge. For a long time I had the same addictive habits as that fellow on the curb. I thought I had a problem, but the alcohol kept telling me that I wasn't sick. Finally, I came to understand that I didn't care very much for my own well being.

I made a commitment that I would overcome my addiction, and began by reclaiming my self respect. I was convinced that I could beat this disease by turning myself around.

But the alcohol had a strong hold, and I would need help as did the underdog, David, in his battle against the giant, Goliath. His came from a slingshot, but also from his belief in a Higher Power. I, too would need help from an external source of energy before my battle would be won.

To begin with, I had to learn how to replace whining and crying with loving and sharing. I did this by adopting a bigger and more positive approach to my healing process, one that allowed me to experience peace, not conflict. The chaos and confusion in my life had made me a prisoner of my own guilt, fear, frustration, and pain. I had to protect against inner forces taking control. It's something that I can't easily explain. It's something I can't borrow or give away, but something that I must use every day to set an example through my attitude, action, and relationship with others.

I have developed a simple way of living, one where my thoughts replace fear by trust, self pity by gratitude, dishonesty by honesty, and resentment by acceptance.

I believe thoughts are like dreams, only they don't last as long. When the thought is positive, the message is positive, and the result is increased energy and health, greater happiness, and a tendency toward success. The result is good and should be sought more often. The opposite is true if the thought is negative.

By using the natural means of a Higher Power concept put at my disposal at the time of my birth, I came to recognize an energy beyond my own, in my willingness to turn things around. This is how I found my own self respect. With it comes respect from others. Today I use it in everything that I do.

Punching Pillows

I arrived early for a meeting one evening, and decided to wait inside. Someone was already there, furiously punching the back of an over-stuffed chair. He stopped when he noticed me.

"What are you doing?" I asked.

"My prayers weren't answered again," he replied, and went back to his punching. Finally, spent, he collapsed in the chair and said, "In treatment I was told that to vent my anger, I should punch pillows."

"What are you angry about?" I asked.

"It's just like before when I was drinking," he said. "My prayers weren't answered then, and they aren't being answered now."

"In the past," I asked, "What did you do every time you managed to acquire a short period of sobriety?"

"Went out and celebrated," he said. "I figured I could handle it. I just got drunk again."

"Like me, you couldn't do it alone," I said. "Do you feel better now, after your punching episode?"

"Matter of fact, I do."

"Why do you suppose that is?"

"I don't know, I'm tired, I guess."

"Do you think your Higher Power made you feel better?" I asked.

"No, I did it myself."

"Don't be too sure," I said, " maybe this is part of your prayers being answered—in a way that is not of your own making."

"What do you mean?"

"Whining and crying is not praying. They need to be replaced with sharing and caring, but it still takes two to make a deal," I said. "Prayer is not like a welfare program where benefits are received for nothing. You have to do your part if it's going to mean anything."

"Is that how my Higher Power operates?" he asked. "He works behind the scenes?"

"What did you expect," I said, "a postcard? I quit trying to figure out how these things worked a long time ago."

"I don't know what I expected," he said, "something more obvious, I guess."

"That's you still trying to be in control," I said. "If you managed to stay sober for a long while, wouldn't that be an obvious signal, to others as well as to you?"

He continued looking at me, trying to calm his breathing. He nodded.

"You're the one in need," I said, "Why don't you settle back and just let it happen? Perhaps it'll begin a trend, and things will start getting better for you. But remember, it's a two-way street."

"I'll try," he said, "I sure do need the help."

I noticed he already looked better than when I entered earlier, and had found him attacking that chair. Perhaps others are praying for him.

It's in the Numbers

The greatest tests of my life as a recovering person happened after I left treatment at the VASAT facility. My first test came the very day I left, when I suddenly realized, that while I had been putting my own life back on track, the rest of the world had continued to ramble on, oblivious to my humble achievement. To put it more succinctly, nobody seemed to care about me and my new program: My outstanding act of getting and staying sober had had no effect on the rest of the world. I was full of fancy platitudes, all the right answers, and a desire to succeed in everything I did, but nobody seemed interested. Where, then, was the reward for all my hard efforts? I still thought I was driving the bus.

The second test occurred while I attended the El Paso Community College in pursuit of my Professional Communications degree. One of the classes I took was Statistical Analysis, a numerical process, that when properly interpreted, may be used in a way that allows a type of future prediction. I heard a news report that stated seventy-five percent of all recovering people in treatment were destined to fail, thereby suffering relapses within two years. I took this report very seriously, and began a search for a way to elevate my own successful recovery program above the twenty-five percent level. How is it possible to beat, or at least improve these odds? I believe I've found a way.

I'm not a gambling man, but I reasoned this way. If somehow it were possible to surround myself with only those people falling within the twenty-five percent bracket, my chances might be improved. Finding these people proved easy. The people attending the fellowship known as AA, Alcoholics Anonymous, are just that. The membership consists of those seekers in the twenty-five percent bracket continuing to perpetuate their longevity through a conscientious program of positive recovery. There is no room for disorienting and negative thinking. I know of no better odds anywhere.

Proven successful since founded in 1935, when the initial membership was two, the group has grown to over two million—that's a society. A society that defies most traditional rules for existence: It does not operate for profit, costs nothing to join, nobody is in charge, and still continues to thrive and grow annually.

We members simply gather and relate our versions of how life used to be, what we did about it, how our lives are now, and what we are still doing about it. From this feedback comes the required external support necessary to establish our own personal recovery programs that continue to improve one day at a time. We all believe we're on a bus going to all sorts of neat and wonderful places, only none of us is driving. That job is left to someone with much greater intelligence.

CTM

From my Marine Corps days, I remember the command, "Continue to march," which means do not pay attention to the ongoing commands around you, keep moving in the same direction. Continue to march, "CTM," is the advice I give myself whenever a possible intervention arises that might trigger an impulse to return to my old ways.

Relapses grow in the darkness of ignorance, and die in the light of clear, accurate thinking. Not being aware of relapse warning signs is one of the biggest mistakes I can make. I must get information, know what to look for. Failure to do this can be as detrimental as denying I suffer from the Disease of alcoholism. Reinforcement comes to me via regular association with the people who can help me recognize the warning signs.

Seven years ago, the annual celebration you know as Thanksgiving, was just another reason for me to get drunk. Today, Thanksgiving occurs every morning when I wake up sober.

So, what do I have to be thankful for today?

First and foremost, I haven't deliberately put any alcohol inside my body in seven years.

And how about my kids, ten grandchildren, and one great-grandchild? They *really* talk to me, and I talk to them.

My income hasn't increased by any significant amount, but I have more money in my pocket than I ever did.

My total outlook on life has a positive aspect to it that really sings. I'm off the pity pot, and wear an honest smile almost without trying.

For almost seventy percent of my life, I suffered the impairing ravages from the onslaught of alcohol abuse. My mind kept telling me that I wasn't sick, but my body knew better. Finally, I made the wise choice to do something about it. Since that time my reasons for being thankful are too numerous to number.

From that momentous time, seven years ago, I have acquired a degree in Professional Communications, made the National Dean's List, Who's Who in American Junior Colleges, and much, much more. My printed words in this column allow me to express how I was, what I did about it, and what I'm like now. I honestly hope these words can help others.

The most significant achievement, I feel, is that today, I am accepted and liked wherever I go, rather than simply tolerated, my disease swept under the rug.

I've been able to do this because I've adopted a spiritual outlook that I lacked in my former days. I've turned my old life around, accepting the presence of a life-giving force outside myself. This allows me to adopt a newer, improved direction along my march of recovery. My self respect has come back to stay. Life still throws its devious interventions at me, but with the help of my Higher Power, I am given nothing too great for both of us to handle.

Today, I'm continuing to march, all of the while doing something I'm not supposed to do: I'm not supposed to drink, and I'm doing just that, not drinking. With CTM in mind, I'm able to accept life, and cope with its terms one thanksgiving day at a time.

A New Life
In my new life, I'm only six years old. I can say this because in 1992, when I was 61, a fourteen-year-old girl gave me the wisdom for my rebirth. I was sick, and this wisdom taught me how to heal and grow.

I had been at the Veteran's Administration Substance Abuse Treatment Program for a time, and felt that I wasn't learning anything. The magic words I looked for to help me get better weren't coming. For years I had held the belief that I could fix anything broken as long as I could get my hands on it. My problem now was how to fix myself.

One weekend, as our facility hosted several other treatment centers at a barbeque, I had the very good fortune to speak to this young girl. Without ever asking her the question, she gave me my answer.

She said that I only heard what I wanted to hear, and that it was important to listen to what others had to say. She told me I could learn by asking for help from others. I should begin by letting go of my control, and just let things happen.

She made me realize that while my hands may be connected to my body, I am not completely in control of whatever happens to me. There is a spiritual force in charge. She spoke the truth. From her words, I became able to gather my own wisdom, and that helped to bring out the truth in me. That day I turned my old life around, and began a new one without alcohol.

From that time on I have been a new person. My new life is much better than my old one.

Compliments Come Unexpectedly

Among recovering alcoholics there is a saying: "Good things can happen to drunks who don't drink".

The good things come in all shapes and sizes. Sometimes it's simply an encouraging word or two. This clearly showed itself to me one day as I waited at the Veterans Out Patient Clinic for a scheduled appointment.

I saw a friend standing across the room. We had worked together on several projects, sometimes sharing the same class room. I noticed that he recognized me, but seemed to be having difficulty identifying who I was. I walked over to him.

"Hi, Frank," I said, "How's it going?"

"Fine," he replied, still uncertain as to who I was.

"You don't recognize me, do you?" I said.

"Your face is familiar, it'll come to me in a minute," he said.

"I'm Bill Schlondrop," I said.

His eyes lit up and he shook my hand vigorously. Then he said three words to me that I will never forget as long as I live.

"You dried up."

I thought I had been so smart over the years, that no one had ever noticed my problem with too much alcohol. Like other people who fall under the impairing control of the disease of alcoholism, I thought I had been clever, and had hidden my addiction well. I couldn't help believing I had become inured to alcohol's insidious debilitating effects. It happened so slowly that I never noticed how much it had affected every aspect of my life. But, as the disease progressed, I kept getting worse.

Reality hit me in an instant. I hadn't been so clever after all. For the thousandth time I thanked my Higher Power for helping me to find the courage, strength, and wisdom which allowed me to turn my life around. I took my friend's comment as a compliment, and saw in his eyes that he had meant it to be taken just that way. He was obviously pleased to see me in much better shape.

We stood there, reminiscing about years past. When my name was called for my appointment we parted, and I carried away with me, a new found outlook on what my recovery meant. Good things can, and do, happen to drunks who don't drink.

An Effective Recovery Needs Changes in Beliefs.

There are a number of false beliefs, or myths associated with the disease of alcoholism.

The most prevalent is that after several drinks, one becomes smarter, stronger, and better looking than anyone else in the crowd.

After more drinks, one now becomes ten feet tall, bullet proof, and invisible to all the raucous behavior.

A second false belief is that only the hard stuff can cause problems; beer and wine are harmless.

A third, and probably the most deceiving false belief, is a loss of faith in the God of our understanding. Us drunks blamed whatever Higher Power we may have previously possessed as the cause of our dilemma. It's His fault, since He never provided instant help for our many demands for assistance. Belief became as false as all the promises we made to quit drinking.

The reality of the chemical composition of alcohol (C_2H_5OH) is that it never changes. Alcohol is alcohol whether it comes from vodka, scotch, beer, wine, Nyquil, or shaving lotion. Once inside our bodies it wages war by slowly destroying bits and pieces of our liver, brain, kidneys, and other vital organs. Given enough time, it wins every battle.

Today, many years sober, my mind and body are still chemically and biologically the same as when I was drinking–I'm healthier yes, but still the same basic person I used to be. I've had to redirect my beliefs in a new, more positive way. I do believe there is a regulating power holding the stuff of the universe together in a more-or-less semblance of intelligent direction. I draw upon this realization, and my support program for my power.

The important thing is that I realize I am not completely in charge of whatever happens to me. Choices must be made, but I deal with them with complete assurance that there is nothing too great for both me and my beliefs to handle.

My old desires, drives, persistence, and feelings and emotions have had to be redirected in accordance with a new and better way of life. A sober way of life. I am one of the lucky ones. I managed to turn my life around before it became too late. I see others not as fortunate as I, still in the grips of the demon alcohol. I know in my heart what they should do, but it is not within my power to forcibly change anyone else. The best I can do is continue to provide a good example. Recovery from the disease of alcoholism is up to each affected individual–with some external help. Believing makes it easier.

One Day at a Time

How long have you been sober? This is a question I'm frequently asked. My response is if the person asking arose prior to the time I did, and hadn't had a drink yet, then that person has more sobriety for the day than I.

I'm also asked if there are any easy short cuts or magic words to help with staying sober.

I'm not aware of any shortcuts or magic words, but I believe there is a speed limit. One day at a time–this is the maximum speed limit for my recovery program. I may proceed more slowly, but I certainly can't go any faster. One day at a time is all I'm given, and this one day is the only thing that matters. One day is enough for me, and sometimes my recovery program requires a concerted effort at smaller increments of time: hour by hour, moment by moment, even breath by breath.

Yet, people are object-oriented. Everything we do is connected in some way to an image, specific time of the clock, or a significant word that signals it is time for us to do something–take some action. It is only human nature to want to tie something as important as a recovery program to a familiar reminder, particularly for newcomers embarking on what seems like a terribly long journey.

If there is any key word with special meaning for me, that word would be *now.* As long as I don't drink now, I have no problem. String enough *nows* together and, lo and behold, they make a day, and that's all I need. My sobriety from the past is great, makes for a firm base, but it is still gone. I can't purchase it with a credit card, I can't sell it, lend it to anyone, or even give any of it away. My entire recovery effort stays in the present.

I love to daydream, and make plans, but I also avoid becoming too expectant. Outcomes of my future plans rarely reach an end precisely the way I initially had hoped. Lack of fulfillment, or disappointing results, can trigger old emotions that may detract from my mission. I don't spend much of my valuable time concerned with tomorrow, it'll get here soon enough, and I'll be ready. Now, is all that matters.

Faith

I needed to kick off the tombstone pressing down on me. My basic problem was skepticism. While searching for the truth, I made many mistakes before I understood. It took me a long time to find the concept I refer to as my Higher Power.

In my search for spirituality, I studied various aspects of different beliefs. Because of my education, and since I'm surrounded by material things, my attention focused on the physical world. Like most people, I think in terms of substance–for things to make sense, they must have corporeal reality.

Not all religions are able to be expressed and defined clearly and logically. There are differences between belief in a set of propositions, and in a faith which enables people to put trust in them. At one point my research seemed to say that God is one of the greatest human ideas of all time, and as such, the belief becomes subject to human error and folly. Some people believe that God does not exist, but that the concept of one is necessary so that we can. Some people believe today, that it is more important for a theory of God to work, than to be logically or scientifically sound. Something is required to explain the mysteries and tragedies of life.

Definitive answers did not come easy. Involved were interpretations which necessitated both material and devine attributes of reason. My searches involved an insight, a sense of involvement, even awe, elevating my mind to a higher level, and that allowed me to know that I somehow understood a little of what it's all about. It became so intense I could taste it. It came thick as lava, but fast as lightning. I have come to realize it's necessary to spend an enormous amount of time just to find that rare moment when something makes obvious sense. I found that human life does indeed contain a requirement for transcendence.

I believe today that I come from the stuff of stars, and whether creation or evolution brought me into my current existence is unimportant. The reality is that I am related to all others born from the stuff of stars, and I must make a conscious effort to relate and share with them. As I struggle with my inadequate efforts seeking to find a way to make contact with a new sense of power and direction, my physical, mental, and spiritual self constantly changes as it adapts to its new surroundings.

Today, I have faith in a Higher Power concept that I don't fully understand, and that's all right with me. It gets better the longer I work at it.

Unlimited Vista

Tears streamed down my face.

"What did you see?" The woman asked.

I tried to answer, unable to find the words. For I had just witnessed a sudden image of how to cure my illness.

I was attending the Veterans Administration Substance Abuse Treatment Program, and in the vernacular of recovering people, was working on Step One. My therapist had given extra hours of time to help me find a direction with my recovery program. She was recovering herself, otherwise I am convinced that she would have had no way of ever knowing that I had "seen" anything.

As with all newly admitted patients, I found this part of recovery to be most difficult. I still blocked most of what the therapists told me. I was convinced that I could do this my way. Unfortunately, my way seemed to be full of obstacles.

Then, in a flash, everything seemed to open up. Suddenly I had seen that there were no limits to where my recovery program could take me, as long as I was willing. I called it a sudden spiritual realization.

In that instant, I had seen a limitless vista, white with clouds, admitting silver-gold sunshine through and through with nothing to block the panorama.

In that instant, I saw that by giving up alcohol, I could open an unlimited new life for myself. There were no boundaries. I could go as far as I wished with nothing to hold me back. All I had to do was ask for help. The realization was overpowering. That was why I cried. I realized then that it's OK for a grown man to cry.

Medical documentation indicates that for patients experiencing a spiritual awakening, recovery from drug addiction is almost always assured.

That vision gave me strength, faith, and the courage to fly to new heights. Of a greater value, it gave me the wisdom to guide me there. I am blessed with a solid recovery program. I no longer need the crutch of alcohol to support whatever it is that I wish to do.

Fight of my Life

Why do we do it? Why do we use the holidays as another excuse to get drunk, fill our jails and hospitals with sick bodies refusing to get better?

It's because alcohol never rests. It waits patiently, and strikes when our guard is down. Alcoholism is a disease that tells the victim he or she doesn't have a disease.

I can compare my recovery from the disease of alcoholism to a prize fight. I've won the first round, but the bout is a long one, and the holidays keep coming around. What better reason than Christmas and New Year's to do a little celebrating? After all, everybody else does it, why not me?

Yet today, I realize that in my case, even the smallest intake of alcohol will spell disaster, and I don't ever want to let my guard down and lose the fight. Many people suffered because of my transgression. Now, I can't recover alone. I have found that as I strive to maintain an honest effort to perpetuate my longevity by shunning alcohol, there are lots of people in my corner to help: My Higher

Power never sleeps, my sponsor is always available, and above all, there is the loving support of my family.

As this year comes to an end, and I continue to celebrate my holidays sober, I gain great pleasure whenever my grandchildren run to me for a hug. I can see in their eyes how much they love me, even though some are old enough to remember how I used to be. This, for me, advertises my own healing in action.

This allows me to get high without alcohol. And the high is a enduring one that I can appreciate and enjoy, not some temporary escape that will dissolve in the morning into the same old denial and cries of self pity.

Holidays don't change, but people do. Nothing is more rewarding for me than to give thanks to my Higher Power at the end of each day by praying: Thanks for helping me to stay sober today.

Printed in the United States
5600